HANDS of HUR

HAVE WE *LOST* The Plot?

Returning to the One Story of the One God

FRAN SCIACCA

Hands of Hur

4725 Caldwell Mill Road
Birmingham, AL 35243-3056

www.handsofhur.org

©2022 by Fran Sciacca

www.fransciacca.com

Published in the United States of America by Hands of Hur Inc., Birmingham, Alabama.

All rights reserved. No part of this book may be reproduced in any form without written permission from Hands of Hur Inc.

All Scripture quotations, unless otherwise indicated, are from the Holy Bible, English Standard Version®, copyright © 2001 by Crossway Bibles, a publishing ministry of Good News Publishers. Used by permission. All rights reserved.

Scripture quotations marked NASB, are from the NEW AMERICAN STANDARD BIBLE®. Copyright © 1960, 1962, 1962, 1968, 1971, 1972, 1973, 1975, 1977, 1995 by The Lockman Foundation. Used by permission. (www.lockman.org)

Scripture quotations marked NIV, are from the Holy Bible, New International Version®. NIV®. Copyright © 1973, 1978, 1984 by International Bible Society. Used by permission o Zondervan Publishing House. All rights reserved.

Italics within Scripture quotations are author's emphasis.

Cover and interior design: Geoff Sciacca

ISBN - 13: 978-0-9859676-3-5

Printed in U.S.A.

P 1

Y 22

This book on losing the plot did not lose *its* plot because of the countless coffee conversations, flurries of emails, and innumerable revisions between my beloved wife, Jill, and Liz Bohlke, a former student, now friend. Significantly, a Baby Boomer and a Millennial were both vested with the success of this project. A testimony to the scope of the threat exposed by the book. Jill's intimate familiarity with my own heart, Liz's passionate devotion to both the content and need for this book, and the publishing history of both women, created a perfect duo of "textperts." It is an inadequate gesture coming from a profoundly grateful heart, that I dedicate this book to them.

Contents

Preface: *Why I Wrote This Book* vii

Introduction: *The One Story and Why We Need It Now* ix

PART 1: The Story Words

Chapter One - *Learning To See Out of Both Eyes* 3

Chapter Two - *Four-Dimensional Faith* 17

Chapter Three - *PEACE: "All Ya Need Is Love"…Not!* 25

Chapter Four – *GRACE: More Amazing Than You Know* 31

Chapter Five – *RIGHTEOUSNESS: Getting It "Right"* 37

Chapter Six – *SANCTIFICATION: Transformed for a Purpose* 47

PART 2: The (meta)Narrative

Chapter Seven – *What's the Story On the One Story?* 57

Chapter Eight – *What Is the Bible…Really?* 65

Chapter Nine – *"Let's Work Our Way Backwards"* 69

Chapter Ten – *New Eyes, Not Better Glasses* 77

Chapter Eleven – *The Power of the Gospel: Narrative or Imperative?* 87

PART 3: The One Story of the One God

Chapter Twelve – *ACTS I–III: Commencement, Conflict, Complication* 95

Chapter Thirteen – *INTERMISSION: The Story's "Missing Page"* 105

Chapter Fourteen – *ACT IV: Climax* 113

Chapter Fifteen – *ACT V: Culmination* 123

Chapter Sixteen – *Adam and Eve Cost Us More Than "Paradise"* 133

Chapter Seventeen – *Would You Recognize Jesus If You Met Him?* 149

PREFACE
Why I Wrote This Book

I've written several books in my seventy-plus years on this earth. Each represented a different season of my life and work. In some ways, this book is a culmination of my teaching. Much of this material has appeared before—some concepts are boiled down; some expanded. A few are brand new. Many ideas are concentric circles of truth the Lord has shown me over many decades of life and ministry. All of the material orbits around what I hope is my life's central legacy: sharing the One Story of the One God.

I started a version of this book nine years ago, and, while I hold to the tenets I first shared, as I've gotten older, I've seen one core truth rise above the rest: The Bible is a narrative. This truth has become dearer to me as I've realized that most modern Christians are unaware of it. The Bible is a narrative more than anything else, perhaps. Why would God take the time to weave together 66 individual books over 1,500 years? So that Christians could formulate doctrines, create religious merchandise, or form denominations? I don't think so. He gave us an amazing and unique record of His purposes for all time, and He even included the ending so that we can have hope while we wait.

As my remaining time to teach gets shorter every day, I've realized that my focus has shifted to this—the primacy of this single narrative presented in the Bible, which I call the One Story. I believe our very purpose in life comes from this One Story, and so it goes without saying—we *must* get it right. That's what we are seeking to do here.

As we embark on this journey, we will ask a lot of questions, hopefully pulling up those floorboards in your heart. For believers, there are Christian concepts (I call them "Story words") that we need to turn over in our minds, hopefully seeing what was always there. Sort of like an eye exam, our life purpose comes more and more into focus with a couple of clicks.

That's where we are headed in this book. My prayer is that along the way you will find *Have We Lost the Plot?* refreshingly honest, prophetically therapeutic, and realistically hopeful.

INTRODUCTION
The One Story And Why We Need It Now

"Story is the bandage of the broken. Sutures of the shattered. The tapestry upon which we write our lives. Upon which we lay the bodies of the dying and the about-to-come-to-life. And if it's honest, true, hiding nothing, revealing all, then it is a raging river and those who write it find they have something to give — that they are not yet empty."[1]

We all need a story. For some, a story to star in. For some, a story to tell. But for most, just a story to be a part of because stories are going somewhere. Stories have a plot, and we all intuitively know that plot implies purpose. To some degree, we are all plot hungry, in search of a narrative. This narrative is created by us, or more likely, by someone else. Who that someone else is really matters.

I turned 70 in 2020. In those seven decades, I lived through the Sixties, the Vietnam War, the Civil Rights Movement, the assassinations of John F. Kennedy, Martin Luther King, and Bobby Kennedy, the end of the Cold War, three presidents facing impeachment, 9/11, and a global pandemic. Those were the headliners, among a list of lesser events. I'm familiar with cataclysmic events, but the past decade has been more volatile than all the others combined. Like a cultural version of the first two chapters of the Book of Job, the catastrophes have arrived in waves, one after another, without giving us time to think, grieve, or anticipate what is next.

The COVID pandemic has caused inestimable disruption in every corner of life on nearly every inch of the planet. But perhaps the most devastating consequences have occurred offscreen, unreported by the nightly news — the total loss of the rhythms of our lives — work schedules, study groups, daily meetings, weekly worship, birthday parties, spontaneous shopping, and gathering. In many cases, we figured out virtual replacements for these life events, but most of those attempts to restore "normalcy" were emaciated versions of the real thing. Robbed of the kinds of face-to-face interactions that nourish our self-worth and frame our identity, we found ourselves naked before the mirror of meaning. With our "markers" suddenly gone, we were forced to wonder who we were and if what we did really mattered. Social media no longer fed our plot hunger. It fed our fears.

COVID isn't the only crisis we've faced of late. The death of George Floyd, a volatile economy, QAnon, gender and race issues, and a bitter election cycle are just a few of the crises thrown into the cultural Instant Pot. Turn up the heat and pressure, and suddenly you're in conflicts with people you thought you knew. Our relational capital seems to be much less than we thought. Never have so many people been so utterly lost, desperate for answers to existential questions: *Who am I? What am I supposed to do with my life?* At this moment in America, especially among the faith community, these profound inquiries are undergoing cataclysmic shifts. Because personal identity and purpose are the foundation of our most basic security, we're currently stuck in a world of insecure people. And insecure people have their heads and hearts on a swivel. They are afraid. They are distrustful. They are irritable. You get a *lot* of people living this way long enough, and you have a culture of anger. That's where we are right now.

I can't speak for America as a whole, but I have been speaking about (and to) American evangelicals for nearly 40 years. I believe the American evangelical church, like the Jews in the 6th century B.C., has been taken captive. Not by a nation like Babylon, but by an even more ancient equivalent—a sinful quest for power and control. This residue of humanity's first sin, when left unchecked, lures us to destruction. It's most evident in modern evangelicalism's push to own the power structures of our day—the machinery of the political process. Christians used to spend their time helping others decipher between right and wrong. Today, they're more concerned with deciphering between Right and Left.

Of course, Christians have always disagreed. Disagreement is the inevitable consequence of the Fall of humanity. But disagreement is immensely different from division. Division among the family of God is the ultimate spiritual check engine light. It is the opposite of God's purposes. It's a big deal. Like a wildfire, it is all-consuming, generating lots of heat and very little light, clouding everything in sight.

Where we are today isn't surprising. Many of these seeds were sown about 30 years ago. In the 90s, Christians were embroiled in what was christened "the culture wars." And a series of books, articles, and conferences dotted that decade. The unfortunate stepchild of these incestuous ramblings was an entrenched, "us-them," "either-or," "win-lose" vocabulary, and a growing number of folks with strong *feelings* about certain *people*, parading as deep *convictions* about biblical *issues*. Keep in mind that this all coalesced a decade before social media. Don't blame technology for where we are now. It merely dropped a turbocharger on a high horsepower engine that was already running quite well.

But this present hour is different. Very different. We're at war with *each other*, and the reciprocal accusations are justified by simply associating other believers with that demographic we're "at war" with. American Christians are divided over issues unrelated to the Scriptures and the mission of the Church. Political party affiliation, mask-wearing, and vaccinations are among the topics du jour. The world watches as God's people quarrel like a bride and groom, drunk at their wedding, and naturally, the onlookers want nothing to do with us—or our Lord.

But what if this time in history is a tipping point? What if this is the most vital moment to be alive, rather than the hardest?

What if, in all this pain and conflict, God is seeking to get our attention? If all that has happened around us, to us, and in us over the past few years is a merciful God shaking a sleeping people as He tries to wake us?

What if there is more than a narrative? What if there really *is* a single story—a metanarrative if you wish—that provides meaning because it has a plot, and it has a plot because it has an Author? And because a story is dated by its author, what if this one is eternal? What if this story is so grand that it is completely inclusive? A story that reaches so far behind the curtain of the past that it fades into the mists of what can be known but also passes through the present into a future that extends beyond death.

What if it has room for everything and everyone—good and evil, tsunamis and sunrise, Alzheimer's and adolescence, childbirth and stillbirth, brokenness and healing, celebrities and outcasts?

What if this story provided enough answers to keep you sane but enough mystery to keep you humble?

And what if you discovered that you were made for a story like this? What if you found out that your purpose was inseparably intertwined with the plot of this story because your very design fits the fabric of the tale? Wouldn't you want to know this story?

If your interest is piqued, I invite you to come with me. You who love the Church. You who have been hurt by it and have grown cold with cynicism and distrust. The fact that you're reading these words is testimony that you're still hoping. And I believe that as you wade through these pages, that hope will grow into reasonable confidence for you to step into the future. But before our train leaves the station, I want to give you some personal context.

First, I've been a teacher for nearly four decades. And as I've aged in that vocation and become more in love with the One Story, I've found myself addressing my audiences with the word "beloved." Especially if what I'm about to say is important to me. It's both a term of endearment and a true reflection of the love I have for the characters of this story—and the ones reading it.

Second, you'll occasionally see me using the Old Testament covenant name for God—*Yahweh*—in this book. I do so very intentionally when I teach to remind my audience (and myself) that the God to whom I pray is the same God who revealed Himself to His people as "Yahweh." He hasn't changed, and as you'll discover fully in this book, the story we find ourselves in is much, much older than the first Christmas. So consider the appearances of *Yahweh* as you read, my subtle attempts to remind you of your spiritual heritage and the origins of the gospel.

Finally, I will periodically use *Yeshua* instead of Jesus, because it's his true name. "Jesus" is the Greek rendering of Yeshua. Both names mean "God is salvation" or "God saves."

I do these things to keep us connected to the backstory of the One Story. Trust me, this will make more sense as we go along, but for now, keep this mental sticky note.

Before we begin this journey, there is a question we, as believers, must ask ourselves: Are we forcing God into our own story? Or are we trying to find our place within His—the One Story of the One God?

PART

I

The Story Words

1 Learning to See Out of Both Eyes

> Clocks cannot tell our time of day,
> For what event to pray,
> Because we have no time, because
> We have no time until
> We know what time we fill,
> Why time is other than time was…
> (from: "We're Late," by W.H. Auden)[1]

My mother-in-law, Bernice Anderson, was an amazing woman. Much of what endeared her to me was her respect for time. Her thoughtfully composed birthday and anniversary cards always arrived early. If you ever asked Bernice if she'd like another cup of coffee, her immediate response was to check her watch. Self-discipline on her caffeine intake! She would have had little patience for our modern culture, being late for a meeting or fickle with plans. "I'm sorry—I just ran out of time," would have carried little weight with Bernice. My wife, Jill, and I still quote her mother's enduring aphorism: *There's always time for what's important to you.* We knew what she meant. *If you considered this important, you would have made time for it!*

It was a significant moment when, at Bernice's military funeral at Fort Snelling National Cemetery in Minneapolis, Jill opened the container with her mother's ashes and tucked the watch inside. Jill turned to me and smiled. "She won't need this anymore."

The image of the watch in a casket is a lasting one in my mind because we who claim kinship to Jesus are notoriously confused when it comes to time. What is it and what's the proper way to "tell" it? For example, how are we to live in the "place" we find ourselves in history, at any given minute, year, decade, or century? What is the Church's "place" in the variegated expressions of humanity we glibly call *culture*? Entire ideologies, theologies, and movements have emerged as a result. A few are still around. Among them, two common extremes: the "separation/retreat *from* culture" of Fundamentalism on one end and the "identification *with* culture" of Liberalism on the other end. But perhaps the two most popular and visible today are the "opposition *to* culture" of Christian Nationalism and the "transformation *of* culture" of what's left of classic Evangelicalism.

This whole notion of time and place is vital in a book that purports to be about plot and story. I'd go so far as to say that our ignorance (or half-understanding) as believers regarding the *when* and *where* we are living has given birth to a quiet pandemic of a spiritual nature. We seem to have lost our sense of purpose, both corporately as the family of God and individually as members of it. That's because *why* we are living isn't clear until we know the truth about the *when* and *where*. To be ignorant of the last two guarantees a loss of purpose, or worse, a deep commitment to the wrong things.

So, before we get to the heart of this book—there really is a purpose for us because there really is a story—I want us to relearn some things that we might have forgotten (or never known). The first has to do with time. Time, as presented to us in the Bible, is vastly richer, more awe-inspiring, and more defining than we've realized.

Here, I want to give a bit of warning. Some of what follows will be difficult. Not because it's hard to understand, but because it's likely going to be foreign. Sort of like what happened to me the first time I visited a restaurant in France. I might have been familiar with the menu items, but because I didn't know the language, I was lost. The same might be true here—but be patient. The vocabulary will grow as we go. You'll get this.

One of the many beautiful things about the Greek language is its ability to provide nuance and breadth of meaning to words that typically are limited to a single English spelling. For instance, we use the same word (love) to communicate everything from our ice cream preference to our favorite movie to feelings of devotion for our spouse. Love, like so many English words, is tasked with relaying different meanings in different contexts. But the Greek language is more nuanced. One example is the word "time." Greeks had multiple words for that concept, but two of them have a special—even crucial—significance for modern-day believers. They are *chronos* and *kairos*.

A mental dash light should have come on in your brain when you read the first one—*chronos*. It's the root of many English words: chronological, synchronize, chronicle, etc. *Chronos* is linear time, and I'd argue that it is the emperor of the modern era. *Chronos* is the reminder that we live on a conveyor belt of sorts. Every aspect of our lives is ruled, measured, predicted, and determined by *chronos*: a Google Calendar alert, the download speed of your internet, the acceleration rate of a new Tesla. We are tethered to time and the devices that provide it. We've also come to value the present over the past—perhaps too much. That's why, according to sociologists, "the news" has become much more than a source of helpful information. It (and those who deliver it to us) has become our source of truth about the world. This is significant because, as professor and author Jeffrey Bilbro put it, "the way we tell time provides the standard by which we judge an event's significance...."[2] Or put another way, if we are living and thinking within *chronos*, what we deem important will be determined by its effect on our present lives. In short, *chronos* can dictate what is significant to us.

This is important for the believing community because *chronos*, as we understand and embrace it, really began with the sin of our ancestral parents, Adam and Eve, in Genesis 3. Because of their choice to disregard God's minor limitation on their freedom, death entered the world. Their disobedience birthed the first actual terminal point for each of us. There are nearly 70 references to death and dying in Genesis after this event!

I know some of you may object to the notion that *chronos* "began" with sin. You'll likely point to "morning," "evening," and "day" in the creation account. The nuances of the Hebrew word, *yom* (day) aside, keep in mind that you and I are captives of *chronos* now and can think in no other categories. Were there progressions of events before the Fall? *Yes!* Was there a sequence to God's creative acts? *Yes!*

I am sure we will have actual existences in resurrected bodies on the New Earth where one thing follows another. But I'm equally sure that you won't need your Apple Watch in the New Jerusalem. And that's not because time isn't important, but because time won't be "time" anymore.

Our obsession with *chronos* is at least partially due to the long half-life of Adam and Eve's choice. The power *chronos* wields is inseparable from that unfortunate day in the Garden. We are stuck with *chronos* and stuck in it. I can't stress this enough. When we lose sight of the enormity of what happened that day in the Garden, we surrender our ability to see all of life clearly.

But there is more to telling time than *chronos*. The Bible speaks of another "type" of time—*kairos*. *Chronos* and *kairos* are considered synonyms, but they have distinctive meanings. When biblical writers wanted to refer to a *quality* or season of time rather than a *length* of time, they used *kairos* instead of *chronos*. The result is phrases like: *time of testing, the present time, the times of the Gentiles, the appointed time, a favorable time,* and *the fullness of time*. These "times" cannot be put on a calendar like Passover or Christmas. They are broad and special, pointing to something unique or important coming in the future. They are almost always something God Himself is directing. Two similar-sounding statements written by Paul beautifully illustrate the distinction between *chronos* and *kairos*. "But when *the fullness of time [chronos]* had come, God sent forth his Son, born of woman, born under the law..."[3]

In this passage from Paul's letter to the Galatians, the phrase, "when the fullness of time had come," refers to the Incarnation—the birth of Jesus—in space and time. Or put another way, the entrance of God into *chronos* time and space as a human being. And we know from Luke's account the specific *chronos* details of this event. He "locates" Jesus's birth in a *narrow* window of *chronos* that aligns with the reigns of seven different people!

> In the fifteenth year of the reign of Tiberius Caesar, Pontius Pilate being governor of Judea, and Herod being tetrarch of Galilee, and his brother Philip tetrarch of the region of Ituraea and Trachonitis, and Lysanias tetrarch of Abilene, during the high priesthood of Annas and Caiaphas, the word of God came to John the son of Zechariah in the wilderness. (Luke 3:1–2)

Chronos time is marked by summer and winter, new moons and full moons, births and deaths, the rise and fall of empires. It's the stuff of history classes and Ken Burns documentaries. This view of time makes us feel most comfortable because it's visible, measurable, and valuable. In our digital age, the entire planet is synchronized, so it's natural to assume *chronos* is all there is. Unfortunately, it isn't all there is. When Paul wrote to a different group of believers in Asia Minor, even though he appears to use the exact phrase that he used with the Galatians, his actual choice of words is very significant:

> In him we have redemption through his blood, the forgiveness of our trespasses, according to the riches of his grace, which he lavished upon us, in all wisdom and insight making known to us the mystery of his will, according to his purpose, which he set forth in Christ as a plan for *the fullness of time [kairos]*, to unite all things in him, things in heaven and things on earth. (Ephesians 1:7–10)

Here, Paul isn't referring to the first Christmas in Bethlehem, like Luke. Instead, his canvas is eternity itself, the entire sweep of God's redemptive purposes. Paul's cascade of "Story words" in this passage is exhilarating, as it should be. It speaks of the redemption of a lost human race, the riches of grace, the lavishness of God, the purposes of God, and the mystery of God once hidden and now revealed. "Time" here has more to do with God's eternal purpose than the Jewish calendar. In fact, this phrase, "a plan for the fullness of time to unite all things in him [Christ], things in heaven and things on earth," is a one-sentence summary of the One Story of the One God.

So how do these two passages fit together? We'll unpack that in detail later, but for now, try to imagine that Luke's *chronos* account fits within or beneath Paul's *kairos* account. Both are necessary, and both have a place. We're the ones who need to "see in stereo," so to speak, as it relates to God and history. If we retool our thinking to accommodate both "time zones," suddenly other passages of scripture begin to light up with meaning. For example, this mingling of mystery and history is the first thing one encounters in John's Gospel:

> In the beginning was the Word, and the Word was with God, and the Word was God. He was in the beginning with God. All things were made through him, and without him was not any thing made that was made.... And the Word became flesh and dwelt among us, and we have seen his glory, glory as of the only Son from the Father, full of grace and truth. (John 1:1–14)

The word "dwelt" here is *skenaō*. It is in the same word family as the tabernacle in the Old Testament. It means to "pitch a tent." Eugene Peterson's rendering of this word in his paraphrase, *The Message*, comes close to the beauty of it: "The Word became flesh and blood and moved into the neighborhood."[4] We can use the word "incarnation" to describe this amazing reality like we actually know what it means—but we don't.

I can say this is a description of the event in which *kairos* and *chronos* became interwoven, but at the end of the day, I don't know what I'm talking about. Beloved, we are dealing with eternal matters here, the very tapestry composed of the time and space we inhabit and that which Paul summarily calls "the heavenly places."[5]

> To me, though I am the very least of all the saints, this grace was given, to preach to the Gentiles the unsearchable riches of Christ, and to bring to light for everyone what is the plan of the mystery hidden for ages in God, who created all things, so that through the church the manifold wisdom of God might now be made known to the rulers and authorities *in the heavenly places*." (Ephesians 3:8–10)

Just as Luke "locates" Jesus's birth in *chronos*, Paul "locates" God's redemptive purposes in the deepest recesses of *kairos*—in Yahweh Himself! But even more startling is Paul's statement that angelic beings (aka "authorities in heavenly places") are being "taught" about the purposes of God through us—the faith family living in *chronos*! If all this seems confusing, that's a good sign that you're getting closer to understanding how much more important *kairos* time is than *chronos*.

And this is not a perspective that began with the first Christmas. The Old Testament prophets were tasked with living within the two "time zones" simultaneously. They wouldn't have called these time zones *kairos* and *chronos* of course, but they had to be thinking and living within a framework that included both. In the words of one author:

> The prophet, like other men, belongs to his time, yet stands for a terrible moment also outside of temporal order: one foot in the *kronos*, the other in *kairos*, his ear to eternity and mouth toward the city, he speaks as he is directed.[6]

The theologian I referenced earlier, Jeffrey Bilbro, takes this idea a step further and insists that Christians must learn to live within both modes of time. Why?

> The standard by which we tell time determines to a profound extent what events we see as significant or newsworthy. Indeed, one of the reasons

our culture has an unhealthy obsession with the news is because its sense of time is off kilter. If we want to learn how to read the news Christianly, we'll have to learn how to tell time Christianly.⁷

When I came to faith about half a century ago, there was a cute little phrase circulating about Christians being "so heavenly minded they were of no earthly good." It was the culture's assessment of believers who had withdrawn into their conclave, seeking to be insulated and isolated from "the World." Unfortunately, fifty years later, it appears that this description may need to be inverted. Many modern believers appear to "be so earthly minded they are of little heavenly good." In our frenzy to stay current and "informed," we, like Esau, may have sold our *kairos* birthright for a bowl of *chronos* stew. We are content (and even proud) to be up on current events without any idea of their relative meaning in the larger purposes of God. In fact, to ascribe meaning to the events of history, especially our own day, presumes to have insight into what God is doing. I'm not comfortable making that claim. *Are you?*

Our divisions over issues of race, gender, and justice have exposed our ignorance or disregard of *kairos*. Political topics consume us. We are so rooted in our own *chronos* that many of us don't even know that *kairos* exists. Our inability to "tell time" has produced an unprecedented divisiveness and disunity. It's also nurtured what can only be called Christian narcissism, i.e., *My life in the present is what's important.* But if God's redemptive purposes flow from a "plan for the fullness of time to *unite* all things," it is biblical to say that our family feuding is contrary to the purposes of God, and in the end, puts us at odds with Him. It's a big deal. Bigger than bumper stickers we put on our cars. It has affected not only how we live but what the watching world has concluded about God from us as a result. And it's neither flattering nor beneficial.

There's an unidentifiable quote floating around that goes something like this, "A man with a watch knows what time it is. A man with two watches is never sure." Based on what we've seen so far, that quote probably needs to be turned on its head: *A man with two watches knows what time it is. A man with only one is never sure.*

We, as believers, should be the people who truly know how to "tell time." We should be the ones who can decipher the news because we consider it in light of the larger purposes of God. We are called to live in *chronos*, but our hearts should be driven and buoyed up by *kairos*. We wear two watches: a watch on our preferred hand that has a blank face, representing *kairos* time, and a second watch on our less-preferred hand that tells *chronos* time. The blank face is both a reminder that we don't know what God is doing and a gentle rebuke that He is sovereign. The events of *chronos* can have no effect on his "plan for the fullness of *kairos*." That's why the psalmist can pray:

> Why do the Nations rage and the peoples plot in vain? The kings of the earth set themselves, and the rulers take counsel together, against the LORD and against his Anointed, saying, "Let us burst their bonds apart and cast away their cords from us." He who sits in the heavens laughs; the Lord holds them in derision." (Psalm 2:1–4)

Beloved, our anxiety over the nightly news betrays a lack of understanding (or a lack of trust) in the unchanging, unalterable, incorruptible nature of *kairos*. There are many believers who think that we are somehow responsible for the eventual arrival of the Kingdom of God in its fullness. As if God's purposes will be thwarted, or at least postponed, if we don't hold the powers of evil at bay. The truth is that even though the purposes of God involve us, and we are invited into them as stewards and actors, what God purposes in *kairos* can never be delayed, amended, or hijacked by *chronos* or by those who think they are in control—Christian, pagan, or otherwise. If we fail to realize this, we will be seduced into living as though there is only *chronos*. Or put a bit more starkly, we'll slowly become practical atheists. The spiritual byproduct of this way of thinking is to assign more significance to current events than the people around us.

Bilbro's insistence that we need to live within both *chronos* and *kairos* falls a few steps short. I'd suggest that we need to first assess whether we believe that both *chronos* and *kairos* even exist. Then, we can identify which is more important—and why. And then, we can begin to learn to live within both.

Before we begin the enormous undertaking of learning to live within both "time zones," another mental sticky note might be helpful. As we said earlier, there is a *quality* to *kairos* time, not a *quantity*. It doesn't have a length. It is not measurable like *chronos*. And to a certain extent, it's not knowable. This is the picture of time that was in Paul's mind when he wrote about God's "plan for the fullness of time" that we just looked at in Ephesians. It was comprehensive and magnificent, but totally unknowable apart from God making it known. We see this in another one of Paul's letters: "Oh the depths of the riches and the wisdom and the knowledge of God. How unsearchable are his judgments, how inscrutable His ways! For who has known the mind of the Lord, or who has been his counselor?"[8]

In yet another letter, he described the purposes of God as a "mystery hidden for ages and generations but now revealed to his saints."[9]

This "mystery" that Paul wrote about 22 times in his letters—this "plan for the fullness of time to unite all things in heaven and on earth in Christ,"—is his summary for everything God has been doing in history to turn what happened in the Garden backward. We glibly call it "salvation," but what that means to us and what it means to God, it turns out, are very, very different. Our understanding of what is "saved" is more a product of abbreviated evangelistic methods than the Story itself. What comes to mind when you hear the word "salvation," or phrases like being "saved," or "inviting Jesus into your heart?" When you think of salvation, do you immediately think of sin and guilt, or a five-syllable word like "justification?" For many of us, these sin-guilt-punishment flowcharts are an enormous part of our understanding of salvation. Sin produces guilt, guilt results in judgment, and judgment results in death. If you want to deal with sin, you've got to deal with guilt. My guilt. Your guilt. We're all pretty comfortable with this line of thinking, and we know why God's solution to it really is precious on every level. Make no mistake, one of the main themes of the One Story is that Jesus is the *only* solution to this mess. And thankfully, he has dealt with it. Once and for all.

But, the sin-guilt-punishment flowchart tends to oversimplify and under-amplify salvation if we only see it as God's remedy for sin and guilt. And theologically speaking, why is this where we always seem to end, rather than where we start?

I'd like to offer an explanation, and hopefully, a remedy. Partial, no doubt, but I think it's worthy of consideration. Just as we saw that our understanding of the concept of time is anemic, I think our understanding of salvation has suffered the same fate—along with a host of other components of our belief system. And I think this all can be traced to which theological faucet we've been drinking out of.

Theology's Two Faucets

I'm going to suggest that much of American evangelicalism has had an unhealthy spiritual diet comprised of nutritious food. And the aphorism that too much of a good thing is a bad thing fits well here. But before I do, let me introduce myself a little bit with the hope it will provide some Velcro for some of you who might be tempted to slide off the desk. I'm a teacher. It's what I've done for four decades. But, it's also who I am. I can't help it. So—at the expense of some of you more astute readers—let me spend a few moments in the zero-entry end of the pool before we dive into the deep end.

In the world of scholarly study of the Bible, there's a warehouse full of concepts and vocabulary that are standard cuisine to intramural scholars but are tasteless to the spiritual palate of regular folks. I get that. I really do. But, what we're about to dive into might require some theological floaties for some. And because we're going to spend some time in that theological warehouse over the following few chapters, I want to put a "big picture" concept on the table first.

In the arena of the Christian faith, we have several fundamental concepts that govern (or should) how we understand God, the Bible, humanity, and our relationship to all three. We call them "doctrines." We order our lives around these doctrines and often form communities with others who embrace them the same way we do. The "big picture" concept that I want to lay on the table as we begin is that there are two "faucets" from which these doctrines tend to flow. Ideally, they *both* should be open and flowing, but I don't think that's the case. I'll explain in a little more detail below, but for now, the two sources of our doctrine—the two faucets—are systematic theology and biblical theology. And, I believe that the anemia we've been looking at regarding our view of time, salvation, etc., can be traced to only a single faucet filling our spiritual sink—that of systematic theology.

Before some of you Reformed brethren start to riot, let me offer some context. My seminary degree is in systematic theology. I dedicated the bulk of my graduate studies to this approach, and that background provided me with a deep appreciation for it. But over time—and I've had plenty of it by now—I have noticed that much (if not most) of American evangelicalism has been shaped by systematic theology *at the expense of biblical theology*. Or at least shaped by systematic theology without the balance and ballast of biblical theology.

Okay, back to the floaties. Let's allow some theologians to provide their definitions:

> Systematic theology is any study that answers the question, "What does the Bible teach us today?" about any given topic....systematic theology involves collecting and understanding all the relevant passages in the

Bible on various topics and then summarizing their teaching clearly so that we know what to believe about each topic.[10]

This concise definition from one of America's leading theologians is an excellent synopsis of a vast field of study. Within that definition, words like "today," "topic," "relevant," "collecting," "summarizing," and "believe" are clear indicators of the purpose and content of systematic theology. It is the construction of biblical doctrines derived from careful gathering and expounding of select biblical passages. A quick perusal of the table of contents of any systematic textbook will yield similar results. You'll find sections on the Doctrine of Scripture, the Doctrine of God, the Doctrine of Man, the Doctrine of Christ and His Work, the Doctrine of Salvation, the Doctrine of the Church, and the Doctrine of Last Things, among others.

Systematic theology texts are also very parochial, meaning that they are for the Church and the churched. And, they can also be quite exclusive. For example, Reformed theology texts are similar but distinct from Dispensational, Charismatic, Catholic, or Orthodox texts. But they share a commitment to the definition above—culling scripture to construct a belief system true to the Bible. The goal is orthodoxy and correct belief. To that end, systematic theology is immensely helpful. A former student of mine (who is now a pastor) once told me, "Systematic theology keeps us from becoming heretics." He was exactly right. If you've received any Bible teaching, my guess is that most of it was drawn from the faucet of systematic theology.

But biblical theology is quite different, both in approach and purpose:

> Biblical theology, in an attempt to balance historical and theological concerns, discerns the overarching 'story shape' or narrative connection between the OT and NT...this approach discerns the narrative continuity running throughout the whole Bible....it does not begin with front-loaded theological propositions or purely descriptive historical reconstruction, yet it uses a measure of both history and theology — under the larger category of narrative— to assist the construction of the biblical worldview-story.[11]

Biblical theology forces us to work out a very different set of doctrines. Doctrines of race, wealth and possessions, justice, the poor, creation, community, and a host of others. Doctrines that have everything to do with living within the Kingdom of God! Not a *belief* system per se, but a perspective on all of life, rooted in the Bible. In short, biblical theology attempts to gather a theological system from the Bible's narrative. This theological system makes sense of the world we live in and instructs how to navigate it to the glory of God.

To me, the most vital element here is that biblical theology starts with the Bible as a narrative. One single story from cover to cover. And because of the immensity of this Story, both in its content and uniqueness, I am correct to call it a metanarrative. Like the "One Ring" in Tolkien's epic trilogy, this is the "One Story to rule them all."

While it is true that we need systematic theology to keep ourselves from "becoming heretics," it's also accurate that we need biblical theology to keep ourselves true to the purposes of God. But the problem is that we have become as ignorant that there *is* a biblical narrative as we are that there is *kairos!*

Because our Bible knowledge has been rooted in systematic theology for so long (at least for the 50 years I've been a believer), our understanding of what it means to be a Christian is at home there as well. This becomes immensely important because, even though the systematic *approach* is rooted in antiquity, our engagement with its doctrines tends to orbit around our personal spiritual life in the present—putting our focus in *chronos* time. But, as we've seen, the purposes of God are rooted in *kairos* time. Our own approach to theology is unconsciously nudging us to keep time with the wrong hand.

So, let's do a little self-audit here at the front end. Are the events in our newsfeeds regulating our hope? Is anger always knocking at our door? Do we feel like the world is "going to hell on a greased pole?" Are we groaning about the life our children or grandkids are going to inherit? If so, we may be missing the second watch.

Beloved, God is still God. His plan for the fullness of time to unite all things in heaven and on earth in Christ is on time. And all things are working together for Him and His purposes. That includes those who ignore Him, hate Him, marginalize Him, and dishonor Him. As I said earlier in this chapter: Even though the purposes of God involve us, and we are invited into them as stewards and actors, what God purposes in *kairos* can never be delayed, amended, or hijacked by *chronos* or by those who think they are in control—Christian, pagan, or otherwise.

Moreover, if we don't realize that there *is* a narrative, then we are adrift from the actual authority a narrative creates. If there really is a story—God's

Story—then we're not free to insert our own subplots, nor are we free to ignore His storyline. Our ignorance of both *kairos* and the narrative of biblical theology leaves us with nothing to evaluate the events of *chronos*. In short, our lives have no plot, and we become a cast of characters in search of one.

Finally, we must continually remind ourselves that *kairos* is the real trajectory of history. And it is a trajectory that can't be bent. Neither by those who exclude God nor by those who love Him. But, it is possible to be on the wrong side of that *kairotic trajectory*, both in this life and forever. And that's because the One Story of the One God has an ending—in *chronos* time.

If we're going to recover the plot of the One Story of the One God, we need to learn the language within it and develop a sort of grammar that includes both vocabulary and meaning. This grammar is drawn from both biblical *and* systemic theology. So, in the rest of Part I, we're going to look at some words that are vital through lines, the warp threads of the tapestry of God's narrative. We've heard many of these words before, so we think we know what they mean. The truth is, the words are multi-dimensional, and we must rotate, reexamine, and even relearn them if we're going to get the One Story right. If not, our faith is in danger of being as "flat" as our version of the Story.

2 Four-Dimensional Faith

When I turned ten in 1960, 3D movies were about a decade old. Films like *Creature from the Black Lagoon* and Alfred Hitchcock's *Dial M For Murder* changed how we viewed movies. Well, most of us. I grew up in Nekoosa, Wisconsin (population 2,500), and the operator of our only movie theater lived nearly ten miles away, so when it came to real box-office hits, you get the picture. Or in my case—you didn't.

The closest we came to authentic 3D was a black and white film called *13 Ghosts* that featured scenes of apparitions that were somewhat 3D if you used the special "Illusion-O" glasses with the red filter option. But for a ten-year-old alone in a theater, it was fantastic—and horrifying. I'll admit I had a hard time that night walking home in the dark.

Like the kid-me in the theatre, to deepen our understanding of the One Story, we'll need to give the Story words that we've learned a few more dimensions. Many of us believers settled on an understanding of these words long ago. Because it is rooted in systematic theology, that understanding focuses on "me" and "us" as believers. Or, put another way, it is personal and parochial. This sort of two-dimensional understanding naturally leads us to build separate, systematic theology boxes for these words. Over time, we add more to our collection, assuming we know what they now mean—at least what they mean for us and those who think like us.

Think of a $100 bill. Most of us know what's on the front side—a portrait of Benjamin Franklin. But what about the back?

My point here is simple. We get stuck in patterns of thinking. Like money, we "handle" these words all the time, but we never flip them over. We may even get a little uncomfortable when someone suggests another side to things. This is unfortunate when dealing with issues like justice and inequality, but it's downright tragic when we do this with our spiritual lives.

I propose we take these "Bible words" out of their two-dimensional theological boxes and look at them more closely. When we do that, the two-dimensional "Bible words" become four-dimensional "Story words." These missing two dimensions are vital for seeing the Bible as a narrative. The third dimension is global (dealing with the unbelieving world), and the fourth is missional (dealing with God Himself). These additional dimensions have always been there. We've just never been taught to look for them. Or we've simply been content to enjoy the personal and parochial benefits of two dimensions.

When it comes to the One Story of the One God, if we look only at the familiar "front side," what we end up with is a two-dimensional gospel that leads to a two-dimensional faith. We put all our theology—our "Bible words"—into their appropriate little boxes and do the things we associate with being a Christian, ignoring the gnawing question, *Is this all there is?* And because familiarity destroys awe, we slowly become bored. The last two dimensions help transform the Bible into a narrative of God's plan for the fullness of time.

The first Story word we've going to "flip over" might be the most recognized word in the Christian dictionary. Unfortunately, it's also the least understood.

SIN: The Untold Story

The first Story word we want to take out of the box is big. It is very emotionally charged for believers and nonbelievers alike. It's a huge word in the faith community and the human community. A quick Google search will garner around 4 billion results. (At present, that's more hits than you'll get for *Jesus*.)[1] The word is *sin*.

I suspect you've got definitions for this concept scattered across your understanding, especially if you've spent any time in church. And, if you grew up in America, you've likely got some ideas about sin from the ghost of the Christian conscience still floating around our post-Christian nation.

If you're like me, your knee-jerk response when you hear *sin* is to go inward. Straight to those places in your memory that are secret. Thoughts and feelings of guilt and shame for what you've done or left undone. If you've had some

Sunday school, the weightier idea of your unrighteousness in the face of God's blinding righteousness is also in your mind. Your uncleanness in the face of His holiness. And guess what? You're right—about all of it. The word *sin* shows up on average nearly once a chapter in the Bible. Verses like "All have sinned and fall short of the glory of God"[2] are tattooed on our cerebral cortexes. We have heard (and memorized) passages like, "Just as sin came into the world through one man, and death through sin, so death spread to all of humanity because we all sinned."[3]

This sin-guilt-death picture is part of our mental furniture. And, somewhere along the journey, we've been told that Jesus is the only solution to this mess. That's why our hearts sing when we hear:

> *There is therefore now no condemnation for those who are in Christ Jesus.* For the law of the Spirit of life has set you free in Christ Jesus from the law of sin and death. For God has done what the law, weakened by the flesh, could not do. By sending his own Son in the likeness of sinful flesh and for sin, he condemned sin in the flesh, in order that the righteous requirement of the law might be fulfilled in us, who walk not according to the flesh but according to the Spirit. (Rom. 8:1–5)

This is what most of us think of when we examine *sin*. We look only at the front side, and we see guilt. My guilt. Your guilt. Guilt is something we pretty much all understand, and that's why God's solution to it is precious on every level. But this is only a two-dimensional view of sin. We need to turn it over. If *guilt* is on the front, what's on the back?

I have a suggestion: *corruption*.

When you think about that day in the Garden, what do you see? Most of us picture two naked people getting kicked out of paradise because of their sin. Adam and Eve feeling guilty because they *were* guilty. That's the side we all know. That's what we tell people when we're trying to get them to consider Jesus.

But if we flip that over and look closer, suddenly everything God had deemed "very good" in the beginning wasn't good at all. Sin's long tentacles spread over everything (and everyone) in every way. The whole universe tilted that day. How can I say that? Where do we find any record of what else happened that day that can be traced to sin?

I want to introduce you to an essential truth about the One Story. To understand it, we've got to learn how to do something we'd never do with a great novel—read it backwards. When we look at the Bible in reverse, we discover a lot about the beginning from how it ends. To be more specific, the best way to understand the fall of humanity into sin is to read the very end of the Story, the Book of Revelation. Listen to this passage from the second to the last chapter of the Bible. It's a description of the end of the One Story:

> And I heard a loud voice from the throne saying, "Behold, the dwelling place of God is with man. He will dwell with them, and they will be his people, and God himself will be with them as their God. He will wipe away every tear from their eyes, and death shall be no more, neither shall there be mourning, nor crying, nor pain anymore, for the former things have passed away." (Rev. 21:3–4)

Here, what the Apostle John calls the "former things" is a partial list of the collateral damage of what began in the Garden. A glimpse of sin's corruption. And unfortunately, the things in this list persist until the end of time because that's when they "pass away."

Act I of the One Story ends with everything being "very good." But the "former things" in this passage are definitely *not* very good. Death is not "very good." Death is always a thief, even for those of us who know Jesus.

And there's more to sin's corruption than simply death. "Mourning," "crying," and "pain" are also on the flipside of sin. These are violent words. Disturbing words. "Mourning" is a word associated with profound grief. It's used in two other places in the Book of Revelation, and it's in connection with "torment" and "famine." But this passage says that when the Story is complete, "mourning" will be gone forever. God says that "crying" will also be gone. The word used here is not like a sniffling but a scream of anguish. It's the cry of a mother standing over her child who's been hit by a car.

The "pain" will also go. Here, pain implies ongoing anguish. The kind that eats away at us because there's no way out. God says that when the end of the One Story shows up, these four things cannot stay. No more death. No more profound grief. No more crying out to God for help and deliverance. No more waking up to hopelessness and despair.

But, that's not all. Sin's corruption reaches wider and deeper than just the human realm. It has altered *all* of the natural world as well. Everything that breathes and moves has felt its sting. Listen to how the Old Testament prophet Hosea writes about our sin's impact on everything else God has made.:

> Hear the word of the LORD, O children of Israel, for the LORD has a controversy with the inhabitants of the land. There is no faithfulness or steadfast love, and no knowledge of God in the land; there is swearing, lying, murder, stealing, and committing adultery; they break all bounds, and bloodshed follows bloodshed. Therefore the land mourns, and all who dwell in it languish, and also the beasts of the field and the birds of the heavens, and even the fish of the sea are taken away. (Hosea 4:1–3)

Here we are reminded that we too contribute to things no longer being "very good." The Apostle Paul echoes this idea, that the entire creation—all of it—is groaning right now because of the corruption of *our* sin.

> For I consider that the sufferings of this present time are not worth comparing with the glory that is to be revealed to us. For the creation waits with eager longing for the revealing of the sons of God. For the creation was subjected to futility, not willingly, but because of him who subjected it, in hope that the creation itself will be set free from its bondage to corruption and obtain the freedom of the glory of the children of God. For we know that the whole creation has been groaning together in the pains of childbirth until now. (Rom. 8:18–23)

In the One Story, all of creation wants to be free of the effects of sin's corruption. It wants to be "very good" again. The Old Testament prophet Isaiah, looking ahead to this day, to the end of the One Story, tells us that the wolf will lie down with the lamb, and the leopard will lie down with a young goat, and a child will take a bear for a walk while her friends play with snakes.[4] That's what "very good" looks like! That's what life is like when corruption is gone.

But if we limit sin's problem to guilt, we miss the big picture. Adam and Eve didn't just get us kicked out of the swimming pool, and Jesus got our membership back. It's much bigger than that. God's plan of redemption is targeted to rescue all His creation from the pervasive effects of guilt *and* corruption. Reading the Story backwards one more time reminds us this is the case: "And he who was seated on the throne said, 'Behold, I am making all things new'."[5]

I want you to forever know and celebrate that the One Story includes you! But it's much more than merely God's personal solution to your personal problem with sin. And that means that the gospel is not, "God loves me and has a wonderful plan for my life." Being a Christian isn't having a "personal savior" like having a personal trainer.

There is so much more to it. We've become entangled in this kind of Christian narcissism (often without even realizing it), but the doors burst wide open when we realize just how enormous this story is. Are you starting to see it?

Using our two-faucet metaphor, a one-faucet view of sin reduces our entire understanding of redemption to a legal solution, one that focuses on the death of Jesus as payment for the guilt my sin produced. In the world of systematic theology, this is known as substitutionary atonement. It's wonderful news — the best news we can receive. But it neglects the first half of Jesus' own description of his mission, which as it turns out, occupied 99.9% of his earthly life: "For even *the Son of Man came not to be served but to serve*, and to give his life as a ransom for many."[6]

God plans to heal more than the problem of personal guilt. Beloved, the focus of the gospel is not us — it's God. The "good news" that we call "the gospel" is so much bigger than humanity. Paul told us that God has "a plan for the fullness of time, to unite all things in heaven and in earth, in Christ." *All things*. And that demands the removal of all the "former things," i.e., the corruption sin causes. And the best part — are you ready for this? — we're part of the solution. Not to the guilt side — only God can solve that, and has, in the death and resurrection of Jesus. But the flipside of sin — the corruption part — that is where we come in, as the visible Body of Christ on earth! We're part of His rescue operation because God hasn't changed, and He lives within us. He's still here.

We're the hands of Christ, the voice of Christ, the heart of Christ, the wallet of Christ, the extra car of Christ — you get the picture. When it comes to healing the "former things" in this life — the things that will be put away forever at the Story's end — we are to be what God is.

And what is God? Well, according to the Story, He's a father to the fatherless and a protector of widows. He loves the refugee and gives food and comfort to those who mourn. He binds up the broken-hearted. He brings people together who apart from Him would have nothing to do with each other. (The parable of the Good Samaritan is a great illustration of what this looks like in our own skin.)

So, beloved, let's rejoice that our guilt is done away with and that there is no condemnation for those of us who are in Christ Jesus. That's what God has done for us. But let's not stop there. There's a reason He's done this for us. As we daily see the heartbreak from sin's corruption, let's view it through an expansive understanding of its source. Let's ask God to show us where we might, like Jesus, *bring* some of the Kingdom to the hurting, not merely tell them about it. Because, as we'll find out on this journey, that's a big part of why we're here.

3 PEACE: "All Ya Need is Love"...Not!

When I was younger, I was going somewhere. It was the Sixties, and like many folks my age, I joined what was called, "the peace movement," never questioning if something like peace could even have a movement.

Peace was a cultural obsession back then. Perhaps the way identity is today. Peace had its own logo, its own clothing, its own music, its own hand signal, and its own celebrities. One of them was Arlo Guthrie, son of folk music icon Woody Guthrie. Arlo had some thoughts about peace and how to secure it.

> All political systems are on the way out. We're finally gonna get to the point where there's no more bigotry or greed or war. Peace is the way. And you don't seek peace, you use it. In twenty years, all that stuff 'll be over. People are simply gonna learn that they can get more from being groovy than being greedy...[1]

It was 1969, and I was a sophomore in college when Arlo made that prophecy. Back then, I didn't realize "being groovy" so you could "get more" was just greed wearing tie-dye and denim. Just because you performed at Woodstock doesn't make everything you said true. If history has shown us anything, it's that it's easier to get peace wrong than right. And it all has to do with where you're looking for peace in the first place.

Most Christians already have a two-dimensional understanding of this word. Again, the first two dimensions are both inward-looking: personal and parochial. For most of us, when we read peace in the Bible, our mind goes to the personal benefits we have with God through Jesus. We love verses like, "Therefore, since we have been justified by faith, we have peace with God through our Lord Jesus Christ..."[2]

We might also think of the promise Jesus gives regarding our struggles with fear and anxiety: "Peace I leave with you; my peace I give to you. Not as the world gives do I give to you. Let not your hearts be troubled, neither let them be afraid."[3] Perhaps we have calmed our hearts by praying:

> ...do not be anxious about anything, but in everything by prayer and supplication with thanksgiving let your requests be made known to God. And the peace of God, which surpasses all understanding, will guard your hearts and your minds in Christ Jesus. (Philippians 4:6–7)

From these passages, it's easy to see how precious peace is to us. Peace was precious to Paul, too. He opens each of his thirteen letters with the exact phrase, "Grace to you and peace from God our Father and the Lord Jesus Christ."

Paul says that through faith, we have "peace with God." The enmity between God and us is gone, thanks to what Jesus has done. In fact, Paul pushes this idea even further and says not only do we *have* peace with God through Jesus. He says in another letter that Jesus "*is* our peace."[4]

Do you rejoice in this? I should; you should—we all should!

But we can't forget that Paul was about as Jewish as they get. Paul never "became a Christian" in the way we understand that phrase. Paul wasn't "converted" like I was fifty years ago. In fact, Paul never uses the word "Christian" to describe himself or anyone else in any of his letters or sermons. Paul never separated the gospel from the Story of God predicted in the prophets and the Psalms. So when Paul writes the word "peace" 43 times in his letters, he uses the Greek word for peace, *eirēnē*. But his mind was marinating in something more ancient, something with a couple thousand years of meaning behind it. Greek was the language of Paul's letters, but Hebrew was the language of Paul's soul. When he was writing *eirēnē*, he was thinking, *shalom*, one of the most beautiful words in all of Hebrew. In fact, in the ancient Greek translation of the Hebrew Old Testament, *eirēnē* appears 275 times, most often to translate *shalom*.

Shalom refers to everything flourishing as it was originally intended to do. Everything following its original design. Or, in the words of theologian Cornelius Plantinga, shalom is "things being the way they're supposed to be."[5] Shalom is a word that points back to everything being "very good." So, in the last chapter when we discovered that the flipside of sin was corruption, that corruption is the loss of shalom. The loss of shalom between us and God is well known. But the Bible also points to a loss of shalom within *ourselves*. The Apostle Paul gives us an insider's view of what this loss does to a person:

> For I know that nothing good dwells in me, that is, in my flesh. For I have the desire to do what is right, but not the ability to carry it out. For I do not do the good I want, but the evil I do not want is what I keep on doing. Now if I do what I do not want, it is no longer I who do it, but sin that dwells within me.... Wretched man that I am! Who will deliver me from this body of death? Thanks be to God through Jesus Christ our Lord! (Romans 7:18–20, 24–25)

But, it's not merely our personal loss. There's been a loss of shalom between us and those closest to us as well. We see this in the story of Joseph and his brothers in Genesis. We're told they "hated him, and could not speak peacefully to him."[6] The word "shalom" is in that verse, but it's there to tell us there was no shalom in that home. Some of you know the pain of the loss of shalom in a family, a church, a business. It's a drain on all that's good.

The Bible also tells us that because of sin, shalom has also been lost between us and nature. Even the shalom between us and the dirt has been vandalized. At the very beginning of the Story, God said to Adam:

> Because you have listened to the voice of your wife and have eaten of the tree of which I commanded you, 'You shall not eat of it,' cursed is the ground because of you; in pain you shall eat of it all the days of your life; thorns and thistles it shall bring forth for you; and you shall eat the plants of the field. (Genesis 3:17–18)

But it gets more serious. It extends to us and the animals. Take this line from the book of Amos: "…as if man fled from a lion, and a bear met him, or went into the house and leaned his hand against the wall, and a serpent bit him."[7]

God's plans for shalomic restoration reach far beyond the two-dimensional boundaries of our relationship with Him and those in our limited, parochial worlds. They also extend beyond the fragmentation within us and the created order. His redemptive purposes reach deep into one of the most needful and yet volatile issues of our day. Listen closely to this "shalomic" language gushing from Paul's pen:

> For he himself is our peace, [Jesus is our shalom] who has made us both one and has broken down in his flesh the dividing wall of hostility...that he might create in himself one new man in place of the two, so making peace, and might reconcile us both to God in one body through the cross, thereby killing the hostility. (Ephesians 2:14–16)

In that passage, "the dividing wall of hostility" refers to the wall separating Gentiles from the Temple area in Jerusalem—upon penalty of death. This passage is undeniably about racial healing in the gospel. Paul first identifies a racial barrier between people, and then he says that one of the express purposes of God in sending Jesus was the repairing of the loss of shalom between peoples. In his letter to the Galatians, Paul said this new family that God has created is exclusively inclusive. Not everyone is in it, but everyone is equally welcome and equal once in: "There is neither Jew nor Greek, there is neither slave nor free, there is no male and female, for you are all one in Christ Jesus."[8]

Considering this passage, should we be passionate about racial healing? Of course, we should! Not because it's sexy or politically correct or a social problem to be solved. But because racial division is a corruption created by sin. Beloved, part of the tremendous divide among believers over issues of race right now is rooted in our two-dimensional theology. "Sin" is bigger than my personal guilt and my personal justification. "Peace" is broader than my peace with God.

Shalom is so important to who we are as believers. Our peace with God is simply the doorway through which we enter God's shalomic restoration project for His broken world. It's the *beginning* on our road to shalom—not the destination. And, according to Peter, it's supposed to become our passion. He told Christians to: "Turn away from evil and do good; seek peace and pursue it."[9] The word "pursue" here is the Greek word, *diōkō*. It's an aggressive word. It's translated 35 times in our Bible as "persecute." Peter says we're supposed to "pursue" shalom. We're supposed to "chase after" it.

And this idea isn't something Paul and Peter came up with. Even in the Old Testament, Yahweh told His people that their own shalom was inextricably tied to that of the unbelievers around them. Jeremiah speaks to his fellow Jews who are captives in Babylon: "Seek the welfare of the city where I've sent you into exile, and pray on its behalf. For in its welfare, you will find your welfare."[10] The irony is that the word "welfare" in this verse is the Hebrew word, *shalom*. We are to seek and work for shalom because we're now part of God's solution!

The *pursuit* of shalom in the lives of others yields the *growth* of shalom within us. If the front side of peace is the acceptance of it, the "peace-taking" if you will, the flipside is the "peace-making."

Jesus said, "Blessed are the peace-makers, for they shall be called God's children."[11] Those who are beneficiaries of the peace *with* God are to be agents of the peace *of* God. Peace-making, it turns out, is Yahweh's family business. This means God wants to mature you and me from being shalom-takers, to shalom-seekers, to, eventually, shalom-makers. Your peace with God, my peace with God, is our initiation into the restoration of the multiple layers of shalom God wants to bring back to His broken world as evidence of the eventual end of the "former things."

This clear, linear connection between our own salvation and the restoration of shalom is obvious in the One Story. Take a passage that all of us know (at least two-dimensionally): "For by grace you have been saved through faith. And this is not your own doing; it is the gift of God, not a result of works, so that no one may boast."[12]

This is a classic reference used to demonstrate that God has done what we were powerless to do. He saved us. We didn't save ourselves. That's *what* He did. But the very next verse contains the other two dimensions of our guilt being forgiven. Paul goes on to tell us *why* God saved us. Listen again, this time in the four-dimensional context:

> For by grace you have been saved through faith. And this is not your own doing; it is the gift of God, not a result of works, so that no one may boast. *For we are his workmanship, created in Christ Jesus for good works, which God prepared beforehand, that we should walk in them.* (Ephesians 2:8–10)

You and I are "created in Christ Jesus" so that we can do the work of shalom because we're now part of the solution to the problems created by its absence. And this was God's plan all along. To create a family composed of multi-ethnic, multicultural, multi-generational people who have been given peace with Him (personal), in order to co-operate with Him in enlarging the family on one hand (parochial), and restoring shalom to the rest of creation on the other (global and missional). Titus couldn't have said it any clearer when Paul wrote about the family of God:

> "…waiting for our blessed hope, the appearing of the glory of our great

God and Savior Jesus Christ, who gave himself for us to redeem us from all lawlessness and to purify for himself a people for his own possession who are zealous for good works" (Titus 2:13–14).

The Greek word for "people" here, *laos*, is the word for a multitude. God's intention for those who've been given shalom with Him is to become seekers and makers of that shalom wherever it is missing. And beloved, it's missing everywhere, in every way. You see it. And you know it.

When you hear peace, I hope you, like Paul, think *shalom*. We are going to come back to this concept in detail when we break down the One Story, but for now, remember this: to "flip over" peace is not to just *take* it, but to *make* it. Once you've taken the peace God has freely offered you, you are on the road to shalom.

It makes being a Christian a whole different matter, doesn't it?

4 GRACE: More Amazing Than You Know

Anyone familiar C.S. Lewis knows there is no shortage of great anecdotes and quotations from the great writer and theologian. One of my favorites is when Lewis was at a theological conference with some of the brightest minds of his day. The story goes that Lewis was walking through a room where others were engaged in a discussion about various religions of the world. Someone stopped him and asked a question: *What sets Christianity apart from all other world religions?*

Lewis, in his inimitable style, did not hesitate. "Grace," he quipped and kept walking.

Grace. It's the short answer to an enormous question. Grace is the one thing that separates the gospel from all other competitors to the One Story of the One God. Grace is the invisible power of the invisible God that can turn a slave trader like John Newton into an Anglican pastor and hymn writer. Newton, after years of blood on his hands, went on to pen the words to a hymn that is one of the most widely recognized songs in the world, crossing all musical genres. One that we have been singing for 250 years:

> *Amazing grace*
> *How sweet the sound*
> *That saved a wretch like me.*

But just like *sin* and *peace*, we need to turn *grace* over to really understand it. I say this carefully, knowing that grace is probably the one word in the evangelical dictionary you don't mess with, lest you be accused of attacking the Reformation.

Let me be clear: Justification is purely by grace. The finished work of Jesus on Golgotha. I bring nothing to the table but sin and guilt. I leave with the full righteousness of Jesus. Apart from him, I'm as condemned right now as I was 52 years ago. Grace justifies and forgives, and that makes it inseparable from the first flipside we looked at— our guilt from sin. Grace is God's answer to our guilt because it's how we lay hold of the forgiveness that is in Jesus. It's a huge word for us as believers. It's a big word to God, too. The Greek word for "grace," *charis*, shows up 124 times in our New Testament, and nearly a hundred of those are from the pen of Paul. He uses a large palette to paint a technicolor portrait of grace. According to him, God's grace is "immeasurable."[1] It's a form of true "riches" and a gift God has "lavished on us."[2] In every possible sense, we are "saved by grace" according to the Bible. "For there is no distinction: for all have sinned and fall short of the glory of God, and are justified by his grace as a gift, through the redemption that is in Christ Jesus."[3]

Grace is a beautiful Story word about a scandalous, lopsided transaction between God and sinners like us. Jesus paid the penalty for the life I lived but shouldn't have, and he credited me for the life I should have lived but didn't.

But this is only the front side. What if grace had benefits for the unbelieving world? What if grace somehow benefited God Himself? What if the flipside of grace looked something like empowerment?

There's an unspoken question staring us right in the face on at least thirteen pages of our Bible. Why do you think Paul opened each of his letters with a sort of a Hebrew blessing, a thing known as a *barakah*? "Grace to you and peace from God our Father...."

Each time, in each epistle, Paul asks God to give his audience two things they already had: "grace" from God and "peace" with God. Why would Paul pray that God would give more grace to sinners already justified by grace?

Some might say these were the common salutations used in the first century. Paul's merely following the letter-writing conventions of his day. Let's be serious here. Do you think of Paul as being conventional? He should have gotten a trophy for being the most unconventional Jew of the first century! What if Paul was genuinely praying that God would multiply grace and peace to them for a reason? As we take a closer look at the One Story, it's clear that the grace Paul's praying about is *not* the grace that saved them in the first place. That's identical for all believers. The grace Paul is talking about here varies from one believer to another. It's different for each of us. Paul wrote to the Romans: "Having gifts that differ according to the grace given to us, let us use them…"[4]

He then describes what those gifts of grace look like when they are put into action. He talks about generosity, teaching, acts of mercy, among others. What I'm doing in this book is an example. Not everyone can do this. I'm not doing it because I'm good at it. I'm doing it because it's an expression of God's varied grace to me. Some of you have the grace to do acts of mercy. For some of you, serving comes naturally. Guess what? That's *not* natural!

The divine empowerment of a person for the purposes of God is scattered throughout the entire Story, even before the coming of the Holy Spirit at Pentecost. God poured out His Spirit on a craftsman named Bezalel in the Book of Exodus, empowering him to perform artistic work as a jeweler, stonemason, and carpenter for the building of the Tabernacle. He gave a man named Asaph incredible grace to compose worship songs and lead the congregation in worship of the One God. He gave a young woman named Esther incredible beauty. Why? Well, it wasn't so she could win "Miss Persia" and wave as she rode through town in a chariot. Yahweh gave her beauty to be an agent of grace to save her people from genocide. God empowered a woman named Dorcas with grace to design and make clothes for others in the days of Peter.

This is the beauty of grace. God gives different shades of grace, and He gives it in abundance. But, God gives it to be *used*. Listen to this: "And God is able to make all grace abound to you, so that having all sufficiency in all things at all times, you may abound in every good work."[5]

What does this look like in the real world? Well, for starters, it means that the "shade" of grace given to me is actually for *others*. You can hear this in Paul's words to the Philippians:

> For to me to live is Christ, and to die is gain. If I am to live in the flesh, that means fruitful labor for me. Yet which I shall choose I cannot tell. I am hard pressed between the two. My desire is to depart and be with Christ, for that is far better. But to remain in the flesh is more necessary on your account. Convinced of this, I know that I will remain and continue with you all, for your progress and joy in the faith. (Philippians 1:21–25)

For some of us, the grace we've been given is financial. Simply put, we've been empowered by God to make money. It's pretty common to hear believers talk about how God has "blessed them" in one way or another in terms of financial success. I've never been real comfortable using "blessing" to talk about money.

Perhaps because of what the opposite scenario implies. But, in the One Story, even this empowerment is intended to be a vessel of grace. Paul makes that really clear in writing to the Corinthians:

> For you know the grace of our Lord Jesus Christ, that though he was rich, yet for your sake he became poor, so that you by his poverty might become rich…For if the readiness is there, it is acceptable according to what a person has, not according to what he does not have. For I do not mean that others should be eased and you burdened, but that as a matter of fairness your abundance at the present time should supply their need, so that their abundance may supply your need, that there may be fairness. As it is written, 'Whoever gathered much had nothing left over, and whoever gathered little had no lack.' (2 Corinthians 8:9, 12–15)

Paul says that God gives some of us more than we need so we can be a source of grace to those who have less than they need. At the end of the day, this means that grace is given to be used—*for others*—not kept for ourselves. Grace is a lot like manna. Hoard it, and it starts to stink. But, give grace away, and it's there the next day. God's constantly shaping us to be conduits of grace, not containers of it. But, for what? For the restoration of shalom. God gives His grace *to us* so that He can accomplish the restoration of shalom *through us*. That His Kingdom may come on earth as it is in heaven.

What might this look like, being a conduit of grace rather than a container of it? The applications are innumerable, but in Ephesians, we find one that's universal, regardless of our gifts: "Let no corrupting talk come out of your mouths, but only such as is good for building up, as fits the occasion, that it may give grace to those who hear."[6]

By the way, there's "corruption" again. The flipside of sin. Our actual words—slander, gossip, anger—can be agents of corruption, or our words can bring shalom. They can actually give grace to people. Paul lived in an oral culture, and we live in a text and visual culture, but the truth is the same. Our words, spoken, written, typed, or filmed, can be fueled by grace and yield shalomic restoration, or fueled by sin, and yield corruption. The apostle Paul captures this dual potential beautifully:

> Do not present your members to sin as instruments for unrighteousness, but present yourselves to God as those who have been brought from

death to life, and your members to God as instruments for righteousness. (Romans 6:13)

Words are powerful things. And grace, as it turns out, is for others as much as it is for us. Beloved, God intends for us to be grace and peace-takers who've matured into peace-makers and grace-givers. And in the process, we become instruments of *righteousness*, our next Story word.

5 RIGHTEOUSNESS: Getting it "Right."

When I was 15, I stood in front of 6,100 screaming teenagers in the Milwaukee Auditorium for the "The Milwaukee Sentinel Rock and Roll Review." It was the final stage in a state-wide "battle of the bands," and my group was one among the twenty left. I was a member of "The Shags," a four-piece garage band that played mostly covers. Before I graduated from high school, we would go on to open for some rather well-known acts of the day—The Association, The Grass Roots, and a horn band called Chase. When I entered college, I played bass for a folk-rock group, "Union Street Fog," which opened for B.J. Thomas of "Raindrops Keep Falling on My Head" fame. Music was the internet in those days. It created a fabric within the youth culture, and I was woven into it.

Music was where I first heard the word "righteous." The Righteous Brothers, a duo of unrelated performers, were poster children for the all-American image of what was upright. I was a sophomore in high school when they released "You've Lost That Lovin' Feeling," which shot them into musical stardom. Five years passed before I heard the word righteou*s* again. The second time it had little to do with music, but that encounter would be the single most significant moment of my life.

Righteous is the fourth Story word we will look at from a 4D perspective. Again, we may know the first two dimensions (personal and parochial) because they involve us. But let's turn this word outward and see how it might be applied globally (to those *outside* the faith community) and missionally (to God Himself). In short, I'm lobbying for a sort of modern Reformation in our theology that is more consistent with the One Story, but also one that benefits me, that benefits us, that benefits others, and even in truth, benefits God.

Righteous is significant in part because it has been in the "Theological Hall of Fame" for at least 3,000 years. But most modern believers cut that short, only tracing this word back a mere 500 years to Luther and Calvin and the Reformation. This short-sightedness may be the reason for our militant insistence on a two-dimensional variation—*righteousness*.

Righteousness is a Mount Everest sort of word for all people in the Judeo-Christian tradition. And it should be. The English word family appears nearly 600 times in our Bible, three-quarters of which are in the Old Testament. It shows up across the biblical narrative from Genesis to Revelation. Its pervasiveness means it's important for us to grasp where it is, what it means, *and* what it implies twenty centuries after it was last mentioned by the apostle John.

As we all know, our Bible is an ancient book. It was written by Jews who lived and thought within the circumference of a Hebrew worldview. Luke is the only Gentile contributor to the 1,189 chapters of our Bible, and even he was greatly influenced by his friend and traveling companion, the Apostle Paul. I alluded to this earlier, but some people might be surprised to find out that Paul lived and died a loyal Jew. This is abundantly clear in his defense before King Agrippa and the Roman procurator Festus near the end of the book of Acts. Listen carefully for the self-portrait Paul paints in the midst of his defense:

> My manner of life from my youth, spent from the beginning among my own nation and in Jerusalem, is known by all the Jews. They have known for a long time, if they are willing to testify, that according to the strictest party of our religion I have lived as a Pharisee. And now I stand here on trial because of my hope in the promise made by God to our fathers, to which our twelve tribes hope to attain, as they earnestly worship night and day." (Acts 26:4–7)

Paul was never converted from Jew to Christian in the way we tend to think of it. My point is that we need to look at *righteousness* not through Western, enlightened eyes but through a Hebrew worldview. We need to remind ourselves that we're only going to see a portion of the richness of this word—*righteousness*—because we're all modern, and most of us are not Jewish.

For ethnic Jews in the Bible, life was understood relationally. Even their very identity was relational. Yahweh never "chose" the Jews the way most folks think of it. It wasn't like He looked at all the people groups on earth and decided for the Jews instead of the Syrians, for example. Yahweh *created* the Jews. He took one idol-worshipping Mesopotamian named Abram and pretty much said, *"Abram, I've got a great idea that I call a 'Jew.' I'd like to make you one. And through you, I'd like to bless the nations…all of them. Are you in?"* Abram responded yes, and as the story goes, "it was reckoned to him as righteousness." The Jews of the Bible existed because the One God had a purpose for them. You and I are the modern beneficiaries of Abram's submission to the purposes of Yahweh. In fact, Paul tells us that "There is neither Jew nor Greek, there is neither slave nor free, there is no male and female, for you are all one in Christ Jesus. And if you are Christ's, then you are Abraham's offspring, heirs according to promise."[1]

So, for Jews in the ancient world, their relationship with one another was inseparable from their shared relationship with Yahweh, the One God. This also meant that life was lived and understood in behavioral categories—how one lived mattered. Not only because it was an honor/shame culture, but because it showcased their invisible relationship with the One God. Those whose lives reflected the heart and purposes of Yahweh are called "the righteous" in the Bible. They are an actual group. That phrase, "the righteous" appears 140 times in our Old Testament, and nearly half of those are in Psalms and Proverbs, two books that deal with our relationship with God and our relationships with people, respectively.

The other major behavioral designation in the Old Testament—"the wicked"—shows up nearly 240 times, and like "the righteous," most of those appearances are also in the Psalms and Proverbs. It shouldn't surprise us that "the wicked" show up twice as many times as "the righteous" in the prophets, the books where Yahweh is taking His people to task for losing the plot.

In short, "righteous" and "wicked" are behavioral groups in the Bible. And which one you were in was evidenced by how you lived. That's what's behind verses like, "The mouth of the righteous is a fountain of life, but the mouth of the wicked conceals violence."[2]

Even the clearest of prophecies about the coming Messiah were wrapped in behavioral language: "Behold, the days are coming, declares the LORD, when I will raise up for David a righteous Branch, and he shall reign as king and deal wisely, and shall execute justice and righteousness in the land."[3]

Justice and righteousness are things that must be executed. They weren't conditions that someone achieved. In the mind of the ancient Jew, "righteousness" was always in motion, and it was always related to the purposes of God. If we don't understand "righteousness" in light of its Jewish origins (the way Paul would have understood it), we'll never understand what's on its flipside. I'd go so far as to say if we get the frontside wrong, we'll reject the flipside as a heresy when it's presented to us. Because the flipside (if considered by itself) can seem in direct opposition to the frontside.

Paul is responsible for two-thirds of the times "righteousness" shows up in the New Testament. It's a big word for him, making appearances in all but four of his thirteen letters; 32 times in Romans alone. It's also clear in Paul's writings that he embraces the typical Jewish understanding of "righteousness" as a *behavioral* thing. Listen to a couple of his thoughts from Romans, his longest treatise on righteousness: "For it is not those who hear the law who are righteous in God's sight, but it is those who obey the law who will be declared righteous."[4]

That phrase, "declared righteous" is how the New International Version translates the Greek word, *dikaioō*. A more recent version translates it, "justified." Our English words "justify" and "justification" are part of this same word family that deals with either *being* "righteous" or being "*declared* righteous" by God. According to Paul, our greatest problem is that we're "*un*righteous" to God. Our lives are defined by a failure to do what is right. A failure to be seen as "righteous" because of failing to behave righteously. To *do* righteousness. Like Jesus himself put it, "Be careful not to do your acts of righteousness to be seen by others."[5]

This is the main problem Jesus had with the religious leaders of his day. They believed they were "righteous" because of their behavior. They reached this conclusion by comparing themselves to other people like themselves and contrasting themselves with those who weren't, rather than comparing themselves to God Himself. Jesus attacked this attitude with a holy vengeance:

> Two men went up into the temple to pray, one a Pharisee and the other a tax collector. The Pharisee, standing by himself, prayed thus: 'God, I thank you that I am not like other men, extortioners, unjust, adulterers, or even like this tax collector. I fast twice a week; I give tithes of all that I get.' But the tax collector, standing far off, would not even lift up his eyes to heaven, but beat his breast, saying, 'God, be merciful to me, a sinner!' I tell you, this man went down to his house justified, rather than the other. (Luke 18:9–13)

Beloved, this is what I would call one-dimensional righteousness. You probably know it as self-righteousness. Jesus says that self-righteousness is also self-deception because the one who justifies himself to himself, as it turns out, is unjustified by God. His self-righteousness is actually unrighteousness. That's a scary thought. One that smug modern believers should marinate in a bit.

There are also several examples in the gospels of what I would call two-dimensional righteousness, which, at the end of the day, is just a bunch of one-dimensional righteous people hanging out together. A sort of tribal righteousness. Jesus put this perversion of God's righteousness on his hit list as well:

> And as Jesus reclined at table in the house, behold, many tax collectors and sinners came and were reclining with Jesus and his disciples. And when the Pharisees saw this, they said to his disciples, "Why does your teacher eat with tax collectors and sinners?" (Matthew 9:10–11)

Jesus' response to them is a citation from the prophet Hosea. Jesus says, "Go and learn what this means: 'I desire mercy [Gk *eleos* - mercy, kindness, compassion], and not sacrifice.' For I came not to call the righteous [*dikaias*], but sinners."[6]

We must not assume that Yeshua came to call "sinners" so he could declare them righteous, so they could eventually become self-righteous like the ones he said he didn't come to save. He came to "call sinners" not just *to* himself, but also *into* something else. We'll get to that.

In short, God has a standard for righteous behavior, and we just don't meet it. We never can. Never will. It's what sinners can't do, even the good ones. We can't be righteous enough, even if we can do righteousness a little. But God has fixed that.

> But now the righteousness [*dikaiosunē*] of God has been manifested apart from the law, although the Law and the Prophets bear witness to it — the righteousness [*dikaiosunē*] of God through faith in Jesus Christ for all who believe. For there is no distinction: for all have sinned and fall short of the glory of God, and are declared righteous [*dikaioō*] by his grace as a gift, through the redemption that is in Christ Jesus, whom God put forward as a propitiation by his blood, to be received by faith. (Romans 3:21–24)

In another place, Paul gets more personal about his own encounter, as a loyal Jew, with this *righteousness* that comes from God:

> Indeed, I count everything as loss because of the surpassing worth of

knowing Christ Jesus my Lord. For his sake I have suffered the loss of all things and count them as rubbish, in order that I may gain Christ and be found in him, not having a righteousness of my own that comes from the law, but that which comes through faith in Christ, the righteousness from God that depends on faith. (Philippians 3:8–9)

This isn't news to many of you. The beauty of the gospel is that the guilt we incur for what we've done wrong is transferred from us to Jesus. And the perfect behavior that we haven't done is credited from Him to us. We are declared righteous by God on Christ's behalf. But don't forget that righteousness is a behavioral category, not a moral one. It has to do with a life lived, not sins avoided.

Why is that important? Because in a very real sense, half of the redemption God offers us has to do with works. Not "works of the law." Not Jewish regulations, but good behavior. Perfect behavior, in fact. In a very real sense, you are declared by God to have lived a life of perfection when it comes to your behavior.

Let me say that again: Righteousness is a behavioral category, and you are declared righteous. Every merciful, compassionate, selfless, just, loving, kind, and good thing Jesus ever did, you are declared to have done. In Christ, you are righteous because you have lived righteously! Can you grasp this?

That means that there is a personal dimension of righteousness for you. It also means that there is a parochial dimension of righteousness for all of us who now find ourselves on the receiving end of this unfair transaction. You, me, and all of the people of God have lived a perfect life in the eyes of God, as a gift from Him to us through the righteous life of Jesus. We get hints of this parochial aspect in Old Testament phrases like the closing verses of Psalm 1: "Therefore the wicked will not stand in the judgment, nor sinners in the congregation of the righteous; for the LORD knows the way of the righteous, but the way of the wicked will perish."

There are our two categories again, "the wicked" and "the righteous." But did you catch that phrase, "the congregation of the righteous?" How amazing is that! You and I, if we are standing beneath the shadow of the complete work of Yeshua the Messiah, are part of the "congregation of the righteous."

This is the front side of "righteousness," and it's vital that you recognize it as a behavioral status. There truly is no additional good that you can do to be righteous before God. In Christ, there is nothing you've left undone. But this is two-dimensional righteousness. And righteousness that stays two-dimensional will eventually become "self-righteousness" or "tribe-righteousness," or both. These counterfeit forms of righteousness are offensive to God. They are the opposite of why He declared us righteous in the first place.

I hope this long introduction has prepared you for the flipside of righteousness. It is a radical idea to modern evangelicals—*works*.

Many believers have been taught that *works* is a bad word. It is portrayed as the enemy of grace and faith. We've heard phrases like "works-righteousness" spoken in hushed or contemptible ways. I used to think that way until I looked at the larger narrative of the Bible, God's "plan for the fullness of time." And what I discovered made so much sense. It also relieved theological tension without sacrificing my commitment to biblical orthodoxy. Are you intrigued?

So we've looked at *righteousness* as an achievement and "the righteous" as a people group—at least the way the writers of our Bible understood it. Now we need to consider all that within the circumference of behavior. Good behavior. Godly behavior. The kind of behavior that God Himself would likely do if He ever decided to take on a human body. Using all that to stand on, let me suggest a slightly different way to view some familiar passages. The first is from Paul's letter to the Corinthians. He said, "For our sake he made him to be sin who knew no sin, so that in him we might become the righteousness of God."[7]

The first part of that verse, I'm guessing we all agree on. It's what modern day theologians call "substitutionary atonement," and we addressed it in Chapter 2. God put the sin and guilt of humanity on Jesus, the one human who had never sinned. But the wording at the end of this verse is important. Paul uses a little Greek word that we translate simply as "so that," but it carries an enormous punch, pointing to a specific and intentional purpose. "For the express purpose that…" might be a better way to say it.

For what purpose did God lay our sin on Jesus? According to Paul, it wasn't so we could have "our best life now." Paul says that Yahweh did what he did to Jesus so that those of us who've tasted the front side of righteousness might "become God's righteousness, in Jesus."

Let me take it a step further. When Jesus got attacked by the Jewish leaders for healing on a sabbath, we read this: "But Jesus answered them, 'My Father is working until now, and I am working.'"[8] When it comes to healing a man who'd been paralyzed for 38 years, Jesus said, you never take a sabbath from mercy. You never take a sabbath from compassion. You never take a sabbath from restoring shalom. This is what was behind Jesus' blistering statement to them earlier, "Go and learn what this means: 'I desire mercy, and not sacrifice.'"

Jesus said something profound to his first disciples around the time of His last Passover with them: "Truly, truly, I say to you, whoever believes in me will also do the works that I do; and greater works than these will he do, because I am going to the Father."[9]

In Greek, the word "greater" (*megas*) is in the word family that means "great in number, size, or significance." It's a staggering promise. When Jesus was in Jerusalem, he couldn't be up north in Nazareth at the same time. But now, with the coming of the Holy Spirit, he can be anywhere his people are. Jesus isn't limited to space and time like he was on earth. That means God's righteousness now knows no boundaries, has more agents and has fewer limitations.

One of the reasons God drew you to Himself, cleansed you from your guilt, and declared your life perfect and selflessness is so that you could become *His* righteousness. You could become *His* mercy. You could become *His* compassion. You could weep with those who weep. You could be the tangible expression of *El Roi*— "the God who sees" and *Yahweh Rapha*— "the God who heals."[10]

We are "declared righteous" so that we can be acceptable to God (that's personal) and find our identity in the community of faith (that's parochial), but also so that we can *do* righteousness with total freedom—maybe even a little bit of abandon—because we don't have to keep track. Suddenly, *doing* righteousness becomes a lot like telling the truth. If you always tell the truth, you never have to remember what you said. If you are given over to doing righteousness, you never have to keep track of what you did. God takes care of that. This is the third dimension of righteousness. The global dimension. What about the fourth dimension, the missional part? The part that has to do with God?

Jesus made that clear in one brief statement in his Sermon on the Mount. He said, "In the same way, let your light shine before others, so that they may see your good works and give glory to your Father who is in heaven."[11]

The Apostle Paul connected the behavior of God's people with the visible expression of God's righteousness too:

> And it is my prayer that your love may abound more and more, with knowledge and all discernment, so that you may approve what is excellent, and so be pure and blameless for the day of Christ, filled with the fruit of righteousness that comes through Jesus Christ, to the glory and praise of God. (Philippians 1:9–11)

But perhaps James (the brother of Jesus) said it best, combining this amazing Story word with the whole purpose of the book in your hands: "And a harvest of righteousness is sown in peace [shalom] by those who make peace [shalom]."[12]

Shalom-makers are needed for righteousness to flourish. And this isn't some new twist on the word "righteousness" or the purposes of God. In perhaps the clearest Old Testament prophecy for the ministry of Yeshua and its generational outcome, a portrait of the sowing of shalom and the reaping of righteousness is painted with vivid color. In Yeshua's inaugural sermon (recorded for us in Luke 4), he quoted from the words of Isaiah:

> The Spirit of the Lord GOD is upon me, because the LORD has anointed me to bring good news to the poor; he has sent me to bind up the brokenhearted, to proclaim liberty to the captives, and the opening of the prison to those who are bound; to proclaim the year of the LORD'S favor, and the day of vengeance of our God; to comfort all who mourn; to grant to those who mourn in Zion — to give them a beautiful headdress instead of ashes, the oil of gladness instead of mourning, the garment of praise instead of a faint spirit; that they [the broken-hearted, the captives, the poor] may be called oaks of righteousness, the planting of the LORD, that he may be glorified. They shall build up the ancient ruins; they shall raise up the former devastations; they shall repair the ruined cities, the devastations of many generations. (Isaiah 61:1–4)

God's plan to unite all things in heaven and earth in Christ, to restore shalom, to give His image-bearers a foretaste of the New Jerusalem, is accomplished through us, the ones whose guilt is gone and whose works are complete in Christ. God produces a harvest of righteousness — of mercy, justice, wellness, and flourishing — through us. Through us, beloved. In this life! And it happens as we worship Him properly, as Paul says by "presenting our bodies to God as a living sacrifice…which is your spiritual worship."[13]

We have been declared righteous *so that* we could become God's righteousness in the world. Hear me say this again: Everything we've looked at in this chapter is totally consistent with orthodox theology. Nothing's changed regarding the complete work of Jesus on our behalf. But what I pray *has* changed is that you have a better understanding of what true "righteousness" is, why it's been credited to you, and what you're supposed to be doing with your life because of it.

If we miss this, we've missed the work God has prepared for us to do. We've exchanged our birthright as sons and daughters of God and coworkers in His vineyard for the paltry counterfeits of power, control, and comfort. We'll see only the personal and parochial benefits of redemption. We'll mistakenly assume that God's will that we are conformed to the likeness of Jesus is something He wants to do for *us*, which brings us to our final Story word.

6 SANCTIFICATION: Transformed for a Purpose

One of the advantages (or disadvantages, depending on how you see it) of getting older is that you get to witness things play out. It's not always pretty, but it's almost always surprising.

Teaching high school seniors in two of the best Christian high schools in the country for over twenty years, I saw a lot of human potential. I was a thirty-year-old seminary graduate when I started, so I didn't realize that "potential" is bi-directional. It can go both ways. I assumed the best and brightest would eventually become the happiest and the greatest. As a young Bible teacher, it never dawned on me that a student could take off like a rocket their senior year of high school but come crashing down by the time they finished college. It's nice now, having the long view on the short view. I think that's called wisdom.

One of the things I recall, thinking back to those years, was how natural it was for my students to view the world in terms of themselves, even when they had the best intentions. A good example of this is when a senior boy and I were tying steel on the roof of a school in Peroña, Guatemala.

"Will you pray for me?" he asked.

"Sure," I said. "What about?"

He told me that he wanted to know if God wanted him to go to medical school. To be fair, that's impressive for a 17-year-old.

"You realize there's something else you'll need to pray for once you have an answer to that question?" I asked.

He looked puzzled. "What's that?"

"Well, if God leads you to med school, you'll need to ask him *where* He wants you to practice medicine. Don't assume it's in your old neighborhood. It might be here." I pointed to the rural hills and the poor. "Or it might be in urban or rural Alabama. The decision to go to med school isn't automatically a call to the comfort of the suburbs."

We worked in silence for a while, but I knew him well enough to know that he was thinking deeply.

Our last Story word to flip is a big one. It has to do with the "fruit" of our very lives—*sanctification*.

This complex word has captured the interest of people from every flavor of Christian spirituality for a long time. Seventeenth-century Puritan John Owen wrote about the "mortification of sin in believers." The late R.C. Sproul wrote books on "growing in holiness," and N.T. Wright is known for his work addressing "spiritual and character transformation."[1] Lots of ink has been spilled on the word, but it's still not a simple topic. You know you're on difficult theological turf when you come across book titles like *Five Views on Sanctification*. So, as we approach this word, we do so with a sense of being on holy ground that's not mapped, even by folks who know more than us.

In the Scriptures, *sanctification* is pretty much inseparable from the biblical notion of "holiness." The Greek family from which we get our English nouns "holy," "holiness," "saint," and the verbs "sanctify" and "consecrate" are all built on the same word, *hagios*. You can hear *hagios* camping out in another noun, *hagiasmos*, which is underneath our English word, *sanctification*.

So, we've got a bit of a broad sense of meaning in these words, and they all orbit around this notion of holiness. Holiness is not moral perfection as it is often misunderstood to be. Holiness is better understood as distinction; being different from something else. Being set apart from everything else. To make things a little more complicated, the verbs used for this idea range in meaning, from focusing on something being totally finished, to a state or condition that a person's in, to an ongoing process that's happening to a person and isn't complete. On the one hand, we find passages that suggest that sanctification is a done deal: "To the church of God that is in Corinth, to those sanctified in Christ Jesus, called to be saints together with all those who in every place call upon the name of our Lord Jesus Christ, both their Lord and ours."[2] Then, in other places, we're presented with the fact that sanctification is still going on: "But now that you have been set free from sin and have become slaves of God, the fruit you get leads to sanctification and its end, eternal life."[3] Here, something leads to sanctification, and sanctification has its own end—eternal life.

So, which is it? Is your sanctification finished, or is it still going on? My answer to that question is yes.

While this might be confusing, the good news is the Scriptures are full of teaching that points to and unpacks *hagiasmos*, or sanctification as we've christened it. One of the things involved is the progressive annihilation of what Paul calls our "old self," and I call our "Adamic residue." It's the part of our ancestry from Genesis 3—the part that loves self and sin and excludes God. Paul gives us both the problem and the solution in his letter to the Christians at Rome. First the problem:

> For I know that nothing good dwells in me, that is, in my flesh. For I have the desire to do what is right, but not the ability to carry it out. For I do not do the good I want, but the evil I do not want is what I keep on doing. Now if I do what I do not want, it is no longer I who do it, but sin that dwells within me. (Romans 7:18–20)

Followed by Paul's solution:

> So then, brothers, we are debtors, not to the flesh, to live according to the flesh. For if you live according to the flesh you will die, but if by the Spirit you put to death the deeds of the body, you will live. (Romans 8:12–13)

In other places, this metaphor of "putting the flesh to death" is compared to changing clothes:

> But that is not the way you learned Christ!— assuming that you have heard about him and were taught in him, as the truth is in Jesus, to put off your old self, which belongs to your former manner of life and is corrupt through deceitful desires, and to be renewed in the spirit of your minds, and to put on the new self, created after the likeness of God in true righteousness and holiness. (Ephesians 4:20–24)

Many other passages describe our lives bearing fruit, because we are people in whom the Spirit of God dwells. Right after Paul gives a long list of sins that are typical of those *without* the Spirit (i.e., unbelievers), he says, "But the fruit of the Spirit is love, joy, peace, patience, kindness, goodness, faithfulness, gentleness, self-control; against such things there is no law."[4]

If we profess to be sons and daughters of God, a progressive transformation should identify us. It is why I call sanctification the Great Reversal. God makes us less and less like Adam and more and more like Jesus. Paul affirms this transformation plainly: "For those whom he foreknew he also predestined to be conformed to the image of his Son, in order that he might be the firstborn among many brothers."[5]

But, the transformation is incremental. It isn't going to happen while we're in the shower or even during our daily devotional time. As we see here, it isn't automatic:

> And we all, with unveiled face, beholding the glory of the Lord, are being transformed into the same image from one degree of glory to another. For this comes from the Lord who is the Spirit. (2 Corinthians 3:18)

As we saw earlier, Jesus took our guilt behind the curtain and declared us justified. It was instantaneous. If justification addresses the *guilt* side of our sin, sanctification addresses the *corruption* side, which takes time. It won't be fully gone until this body's been replaced. So, in the meantime, according to Paul, we "press on to make it our own because Christ Jesus has made us his own."[6] Listen to Paul's charge to the Philippians:

> Therefore, my beloved, as you have always obeyed, so now, not only as in my presence but much more in my absence, work out your own salvation with fear and trembling, for it is God who works in you, both to will and to work for his good pleasure. (Philippians 2:12–13)

Paul's charge here about "working out" is a command with no end in sight in the Greek. Why? Because God is working in you to change your desires to match His! It's a work in progress. This dismantles the notion that a Christian is someone who has "invited Jesus into his heart and is going to heaven." That view of Christian identity needs a proper funeral. It reduces faith to a moment at the beginning and a twinkling of an eye at the end, but it leaves out everything in between—*our entire life on earth*!

Getting this right also lays to rest the popular Christian notion that "God loves me and has a wonderful plan for my life." This soundbite not only inverts our purpose as believers, but it also warps our expectations for life as a Christian. Sanctification is surely a good thing, but it's not always fun. Getting Adam out of me has taken God over five decades, and there's still plenty of him in there.

So that leaves us with a question: "Why would God want to transform me to increasingly resemble His Son — *in this life?*" Is it for you to have more joy, more peace…a better prayer life? Is it so that you're a wonderful person to be around at church? So you'll be more generous and patient? Less angry and prideful?

Yes — there are personal and parochial benefits to sanctification. You and I are much happier when we're living the way God originally designed us to live — in fellowship with Him and everything around us. There is great personal fulfillment in living shalomically.

There's also tremendous corporate benefit when God's children act more like their elder brother, Jesus, than their ancient father, Adam. We all benefit when each of us is cooperating with God in the Great Reversal. Unfortunately, these personal and parochial benefits in *chronos* time have become our sole focus in sanctification. It even seems to be the primary focus in seminary teaching on this topic. Listen to this summary at the end of 17 pages on sanctification in a major systematic theology textbook:

> It would not be right to end our discussion without noting that sanctification brings great joy to us. The more we grow in likeness to Christ, the more we will personally experience the "joy" and "peace" that are part of the fruit of the Holy Spirit, and the more we will draw near to the kind of life that we will have in heaven.[7]

But all of this is only the front side of sanctification, rooted in *chronos*.

What if, in the plan of God, your sanctification had a larger purpose in *kairos* time? What if your sanctification wasn't for you? What if the needs of others and the glory of God was as much (if not more) important than your own peace and joy? What if, on the flipside of sanctification, there was *ministry*?

Let's unpack a statement we looked at earlier:

> "Do not present your members to sin as instruments for unrighteousness, but present yourselves to God as those who have been brought from death to life, and your members to God as instruments for righteousness." (Romans 6:13)

Here, Paul's use of the word "members" needs to be understood as our body parts, or at least, our physical bodies. This is a startling and powerful metaphor. A few verses later, Paul will draw in the metaphors of marriage and the fruit of sexual unions. In Romans 6 and 7, Paul is teaching that believers can bear fruit for God, or bear fruit for Satan, in a sense. We are the current incarnation of Jesus. We are God's children, filled with God's Spirit, tasked with God's shalomic mission. We are the dwelling place of God in real time. This ties in with what we saw with grace. God empowers us because He intends for us to be His presence on earth, and He is committed to progressively transforming us. But, we can be vehicles of corruption as well. This is mysterious and not something I claim to understand, but, beloved, it's true.

So what's this all got to do with you and me? I would suggest that it begins with a renovation of our perspective. When we are walking in fellowship with God, He wants us to bring *Him* into the world of hurting people. The unseen, invisible, intangible God wants to be seen, heard, and felt. Through us, the justice of God gets expressed in space and time. The mercy of God takes on flesh. The love of God takes on hands. The voice of God speaks out. God becomes present in the world of people.

The Kingdom of God is again in our midst. *This* is the "good news"—the gospel—Jesus announced in his inaugural sermon. Do you see this? As you and I are progressively transformed into the likeness of the One who touched, taught, and healed, the world is affected. Fruit is born, and God is glorified. True ministry is at the heart of God's purposes for our sanctification. God is not interested in purifying and transforming a bunch of folks so they can hang out together and slowly begin to become suspicious and critical of everyone who's not part of the group. No, He's told us why He's doing this: "…to purify for himself a people for his own possession who are zealous for good works."[8]

Perhaps some of the best commentary on the relationship between my own sanctification and the lives of others is found in an obscure statement Paul made to a depressed young pastor named Timothy: "Therefore, if anyone cleanses himself from what is dishonorable, he will be a vessel for honorable use, set apart as holy (*hagiazō*), useful to the master of the house, ready for every good work."[9]

The word "cleanse" is a word for purification, and it's akin to this whole notion of sanctification. God's endgame is becoming a sanctified vessel to be put into the hand of the Master for every possible good work. This is God's desire for you, that you'd resemble Jesus, that Jesus would truly be the firstborn among *many* brethren. But His larger desire is the restoration of shalom to all the places from which it has been stolen or vandalized. His desire is that your life would become a conduit from the realm of God Himself in *kairos* time into the *chronos* world that is now captured and tortured by sin. That world of people who were made in His likeness but do not realize it. That world of people desperate for shalom with God and others but do not know where to find it.

Of course, it's much easier if we keep to ourselves and "encourage one another" rather than wade into the lives of broken people. Sanctification isn't always enjoyable, and it certainly isn't for sissies. It's often an upstream journey in a downstream world. But, if we claim God is our Father, we're called to join Him in the family business.

As we conclude our discussion on Story words, my hope is that in each case, you have cultivated a multi-dimensional understanding that has pushed you beyond the circumference of self and similar. And again, I wholeheartedly believe that the "front side" to each of these words is true and personally dear to us. But our theology, like our Lord, must be multi-dimensional. Picture each of these words like sides of a coin. When you spin a coin, the sides disappear and what you see looks more like a ball. That's a multi-dimensional perspective.

Beloved, praise God that there is more than *us* in our theology! So, as we go forward, let us remember...

- Sin has two sides: guilt *and* corruption.
- Peace has two sides: peace-taking *and* peace-making.
- Grace has two sides: grace that saves *and* grace that serves.
- Righteousness has two sides: righteousness *to* me and *from* me (works).
- Sanctification has two sides: transformation *within* me and *through* me (ministry).

As we have seen throughout this section, we must approach this One Story knowing that there is more than meets the eye. We must concede to the mystery that something can be many things at once. Time is both *chronos* and *kairos*; theology is both biblical and systematic; the Story words have different meanings, depending on if they are inwardly (2D) or outwardly (4D) applied. Like the eye exam motif I mentioned at the beginning, just when we think we "see" a certain concept clearly enough, changing the lens brings more clarity. That is the place we needed to be—in the examiner's chair.

But now, let's get up from that chair with better vision and begin to look clearly at the great narrative, the One Story of the One God. Our goal? To be gripped by its beauty and enormity—and to find our place within it.

PART II
The (meta) Narrative

# What's the Story on the One Story?

Thus far, we've spent a lot of time talking about narrative. We've crafted a grammar of sorts, a group Story words and meanings that created a shared roadway down which we'll travel. We saw how much of our spiritual understanding has become rooted in personal and parochial benefits, leaving us with a theology and practice focused on ourselves and an anemic understanding of what to do with our lives. In short, it's possible to live your whole life "being a Christian," but that life has little to do with the purposes of God. Or put another way—one that fits well in our modern era—it's possible to be a professing Christian, but a practicing postmodernist. It's been said that postmodernism, at its core, is incredulity towards a metanarrative.[1] The belief that there is no single storyline that gives meaning to life. The tragic truth is that a believer who doesn't *know* the metanarrative of scripture has no advantage over a postmodernist unbeliever who denies there actually is one. And too often, the two have more in common than they know.

Beloved, that thought should take your breath away.

When it comes to God's One Story, His grand metanarrative, many of us have a similar short-sightedness. Instead of focusing too *much* on ourselves, this time, we focus too *little*. We leave ourselves out of the story. The Bible on our desk gathers dust as we fail to realize that this story is not just *for* us—it *includes* us. But before we get to the specifics, let's establish why stories even matter. Humans seem hardwired to believe that there is a grand plot, and that plot has a place for our lives within it. It is in our DNA to look for bigger meaning.

Stories help us form meaning. They inspire hope. They provide insight. They validate our longings.

This longing is not a new thing. Thirty centuries ago, a brilliant thinker and writer determined to find "the point" to life. His quest took him down many predictable roads: pleasure, learning, travel, writing, architecture, wealth, status, power, love, and so on. He kept a record of where he landed on each journey. His pen name was Koheleth (the Preacher)[2], but many modern Christian scholars think he was King Solomon[3]. Though his journey for answers was long and convoluted, his book was not. His poetic "journal"—the Old Testament book of Ecclesiastes—spanned about eleven pages, including thirty-two questions on timeless topics: wisdom and folly, the value of work, the nature of love, the purpose of life, the certainty of death, and others.

For all his various escapades, our existential explorer made a single discovery. A lament he repeated every six verses on average: "Meaningless, meaningless, all is meaningless." Solomon sought the meaning of life "under the sun"—a euphemism for marginalizing God—but came up empty. And his cry, "meaningless," is the fruit of a broken heart. All he had to show for his trotting was a collection of dead ends—a library of unfinished autobiographies.

Fast forward 3,000 years. Nothing's changed. We are still on the same treadmill as Solomon. You might argue that current stresses that come with living during a pandemic have turned up the volume on this kind of gut-wrenching search for purpose. The countless self-help books that clutter bookstore windows year after year attest to the mirage-like nature of meaning—and the human desire to find it. And this is true for believers and nonbelievers alike.

In 1972, two years after my conversion from pseudo-atheism to Christianity, I came across a statement made by Gordon Dahl that galvanizes the unsettling algorithm: "no plot = no purpose."

> Most middle-class Americans tend to worship their work, work at their play, and to play at their worship. As a result, their meanings and values are distorted. Their relationships disintegrate faster than they can keep them in repair, and their lifestyles resemble a cast of characters in search of a plot.[4]

Dahl's assessment is a modern argument that the inversion of our values leads to the same sort of futile wandering we saw in Solomon's quest.

This rang true in my own life. In 1969, as a young, angry atheist looking for my "point" in the world of academia, I had an existential train wreck. Like many around me, I tried to weave a personal narrative in the halls of higher education. But instead of a beautiful tapestry of coherent ideas, all I got was a conflicting interdisciplinary mess. The ideas from the various departments were not only incompatible, they were mutually exclusive. They couldn't all be true, much less somehow fit into a larger whole. Instead of a narrative, I found a multinarrative. As a young man, I had listened to the adults in my world and came away with more questions than answers. I looked at the personal lives of those same people and found less hope. Dismissal for sexual misconduct, suicide, and embezzlement of funds were among the wreckage of my professors trying to live out their existentialism.

In retrospect, my disillusionment exposed my inherent human need for the dots to connect. For "life" to make sense. And I wasn't alone. Then or now. You know this too, don't you? Our longing is for plot: to find one or create one. Sometimes we resort to mimicking, fabricating, or hijacking one. But at the end of the day, we want one — we're going to have one! Dahl makes a clear connection between plot and meaning. As I said, it's algorithmic.

What we call "purpose" or "meaning" hinges on plot because purpose is dependent upon non-randomness, the deep assurance that life is unfolding, not merely happening. We all intuitively know that there's no purpose to randomness. That's why car wrecks are called "accidents," *not* "encounters." Accidents "happen," but life unfolds.

This inseparable connection between design and purpose extends even into the natural world. Order in the natural world is breathtaking, but scientifically, it has no inherent purpose, even though it has amazing function. Snowflakes are beautiful (and even useful), but they're not purposeful. They're random acts of chemistry and physics. But in the eyes of believers, all of nature, and especially humanity bear God's signature. We call that the *imago Dei*, the image of God. And this God who claims to have disclosed Himself in the Bible is relational as well as rational. You start believing stuff like this, and things become deep quickly.

Using these optics, a rational and relational God, non-randomness, and the idea of purpose all converge in the world of narrative. Of a plot. A story. Or, because God is involved, a metanarrative. So, we have at least a partial answer to why humans have a penchant for purpose when looking at our design. It's because of the *imago Dei* — the image of God — we were created in the likeness of a purposeful God.

Examining the metanarrative in the Bible, we see order, sequence, beauty, hierarchy, and interdependence. Even a cursory reading of the first two chapters of Genesis provides a sense of movement; the specific details play a part, each fading as the next appears. The entrance of humanity is the obvious apex of the Creation narrative. But that is just the beginning. The creation of Adam and Eve is the prequel to their sin and need for rescue (which become dominant themes throughout the rest of the Bible). This need for metanarrative became part of our DNA way back then, and it's part of life for all of us now, whether we know it or not. We see it everywhere in the world of print. Fiction authors, like the late Tony Hillerman and his daughter Anne, are excellent examples. Writing mysteries portraying Navajo culture and mythology, they accurately present the Diné (Navajo people) who are inseparably connected to their own origin stories with a calling to "walk in beauty," which means to live a life consistent with their narrative.

But even more than fiction, plot hunger is evident in the entertainment industry. There are countless examples of movies built upon plot and the meaninglessness and evil when one is missing or contrived. A poster child for this is *The Matrix*, released back in 1999. In the movie, there are two plots at play: one in real time and a second artificial, virtual plot downloaded into humans living in the electronic chrysalises created by an evolved computer known as "The Matrix." The movie was groundbreaking. The notion of a virtual plot that sucked us in didn't just entertain us, it frightened us because of its plausibility. Sure, we could say, "It's just a movie," but look at where we are two decades later. We scavenge social media posts and newsfeeds and binge-watch on Netflix. Why do we do this? What is it in the world of the plot—the pull of narrative—that keeps us coming back, hour after hour, night after night?

I believe the answer is that we are divinely hardwired to make sense of things. We *need* to know that the profusion of points on the radar of life is connected, not random. Whether cancer or adolescence, we need the assurance that there's a beginning and an end. That there's *continuity* from one to the other. In short, we need to know that there is a plot—or, put another way, that this thing we call life has a trajectory.

A great way of understanding this is to revisit our tapestry metaphor. Tapestries are made up of two kinds of threads. The *warp* threads run from top to bottom of the roll, and the *weft* threads run from side to side. In a fabric like cotton, both types of threads are visible, but a tapestry is different. Its beauty comes from the colors in the weft threads (which are visible), and its strength comes from the warp threads (which are not visible). In the story world, the plot serves as the warp threads, supplying direction and purpose—elements that might be missed by all but the one who created it. But the visible weft threads—the narrative—unfold before us in the details, e.g., the names, cities, events, emotions, and personalities. A plot provides structure, and a narrative provides beauty. Reaching back to our opening chapter, we see this tie in with *chronos* and *kairos*. In a very real way, *kairos* is the warp of life and *chronos* the weft. Both parts are necessary, but narrative is where we really live because it's all we can see. But—and it's a big but!—what I'm arguing for in this book is that the true metanarrative, the One Story of the One God, is running on *kairos* time and employing *chronos* time in the process.

Applying this tapestry metaphor to life itself, there are only three possibilities regarding the weaving together of plot and narrative. And they can't all be valid because they're mutually exclusive.

Life's Three Plot Possibilities

The first possibility we've already visited. It's the dismal reality that there really *is* no plot. What we *think* is a metanarrative or "Story" is merely the accumulative chronicles of what was happening at any given point in time. We give it a variety of labels, like "history," "sociology," or "anthropology." But when all's said and done, it's just information. Data to be collated, stored on Google's servers, and mined for its usefulness, sorted by the relevance algorithm. As evolutionary biologist Richard Dawkins preaches, life has no design—only structure, order, and movement. It turns out life isn't a tapestry but a patchwork quilt of unrelated pieces sewn together. There's form and beauty—even function—but no script. No plot. Therefore, it is random, not linear, and has no inherent design or plot. But if design determines purpose, a world lacking a plot becomes a world lacking a purpose. And this becomes more personal and serious very quickly. If life has no purpose, and you're alive, then you have no purpose. This, as Solomon found, is a life distilled down to the bumper sticker: "Meaningless, meaningless, meaningless."

So, if there's no plot to be a part of, what do we do? Well, party till our eyes bleed, I guess. No plot…no purpose…no point. Hedonism is definitely allowed here. It's even promoted. Maybe the Eagles were right in 1972 when they sang, *"Take it easy, take it easy, don't let the sound of your own wheels drive you crazy. Lighten up while you still can. You don't have to understand. Just find a place to take your stand…and take it easy.*"[5]

The second possibility is that there *can* be a narrative. *Yours!* The real meta-narrative (the real grand Story that gives meaning and purpose to your life) is the one *you* decide, based on what's important to *you*. You create the plot. You weave the tapestry using the threads that you value. A sort of self-hosted reality show. *You* get to write the script *and* be the star. Remember the "Choose Your Own Adventure" stories? Well, this is *your* adventure, and that's what gives it value! Imagine being able to ad-lib a storyline in which your most significant strengths or achievements are the most valuable commodities on earth. You'd have purpose, meaning, and you'd be happy. Or, if you're more of a "dark drama" fan, then your pain, sorrow, and feelings of victimization and neglect (the "unfairness" of life) can become the central themes of your story. And because victimhood is the new notoriety, you'd get noticed. In either case, your task is to "brand" yourself so people can find you on Instagram, Snapchat, or TikTok. Narcissism is definitely allowed here. Social media companies depend on it.

This sound okay so far, but there's a catch. You're responsible for all of it. All of it. You carry the weight of your own purpose. You're responsible for maintaining an exciting narrative, and you have some responsibility for the existential safety of the other people you've pulled into your story. And, unless you choose to end your own life, you have no idea (or control over) how your story ends. And it's no secret that a narrative's ending is the thing that gives meaning to the Story.

This option works great…until it doesn't. No sane person writes pain, disappointment, and suffering into their own narrative. We can all list the pain in our stories, either experienced or witnessed. For me, it was meeting the five-year-old Guatemalan orphan rescued from the horrors of sexual abuse. Or talking with a former student who was suddenly widowed at thirty years old during what should have been the happiest season of his life. I can't picture myself telling either one of them to take charge of their lives and "start a new chapter in their adventure." The longer you live, the more you realize that life is not always adventurous. It can be torturous. And during those trying times, you don't get to "choose" how you want it to play out, much less infuse it with meaning while it is unfolding.

To make matters worse, this second plot option also results in a plethora of narratives. Rather than a single metanarrative, we are left with a "multinarrative" where one person's story is as good as any other. But that also has proven unworkable because "just as good as" quickly degenerates to "much better than," and folks are marching in the streets. I know this seems like an infinite grasp of the obvious, but unity is impossible in a multinarrative world, regardless of how many symbols you add to your bumper sticker or letters to your acronym.

Enter the third possibility regarding plot: There really *is* a metanarrative that makes sense of life as we know it. A story worth knowing, telling, and retelling. A story that is adequate but not exhaustive. It has enough information to keep us sane but not enough to allow us to believe we know everything. A story that can simultaneously give us hope without making us arrogant. A story that has a place for everything, except hedonism and narcissism, of course. A story full of surprises but leaves no loose ends—a story you were designed for. Who you are fits the fabric of the tale. And since design determines purpose, getting *this* right is enormous for our individual sense of purpose, as well as the larger existential question of the meaning of life itself. And best of all, what if this grand story, this comprehensive metanarrative, belongs to God Himself? What if *He* has a story? What if *He* has a "plan or storyline for the fullness of time, to unite all things in heaven and earth in Christ?" What if there really is such a thing as the One Story of the One God?

Well, look at that! We've circled back to where we started. Sort of, but not quite. I had to take us on that roundtrip to get us to the door we must walk through next. We've got to dive a little deeper into the context of narrative. This might raise your blood pressure a little, so sit down. Breathe.

Looking back then, each of us *needs* a story. We get that now. And we also understand that if we don't pursue the One Story, we're left with the burden of generating our own or submitting to Solomon's conclusion—*meaningless*. Unfortunately, we are also living at a time when the concept of narrative itself is being deconstructed. And I'm not just talking about the war between moderns and postmoderns. It's a mindset that has become environmental. We live with it, and its transparent effects on us go unnoticed and unaddressed. Basically, the stories keep getting spliced: a 280-character tweet, a 60-second Instagram clip. Our smart phones have made us inattentive scrollers, and Google has become synonymous with the quest for answers. Its modus operandi—to get users in and out quickly—has created a society of people who are proficient at skimming but unable to engage deeply with a single story. Screens are more pleasurable than books. We've become a culture of glancers. In the words of one astute observer, we are characterized by "CPA," constant partial attention.[6] The combined effect of all this is a slow erosion of the value of narrative itself. We can't think in terms of a grand narrative because we have been conditioned not to think about a single thing for more than a few seconds. We have lost the ability to go deep.

Acclaimed technology writer Nicholas Carr, in speaking of an unintended consequence of Google's obsession to digitize books and make all knowledge searchable, also indirectly predicts the death of narrative:

> To make a book discoverable and searchable online is also to dismember it. The cohesion of its text, the linearity of its argument or narrative as it flows through scores of pages, is sacrificed.[7]

Carr calls this approach to reading, which Google provides in broad bandwidth at high speed, the "strip mining of 'relevant content' [which] replaces the slow excavation of meaning."[8] Without realizing it, Carr is addressing the enormous principle that meaning depends on narrative. And what he is asserting about what Google has done to books is true about life.

Carr's assessment of Google should be extremely disconcerting to Christians who maintain that life is purposeful and linear. We believe that there was a beginning, and there will be an end to life as we know it. That there is, to use the biblical vernacular, a "present life" and a "life to come." Even more important, we believe that there is unbroken continuity between the two. And this is the very fabric of narrative. A place for *chronos* and *kairos*.

What does this mean for Christians? It means we must make sure both "faucets" are running wide open regarding our relationship with scripture. Because the Bible is God's narrative (not ours), *all* the content is "relevant." Unfortunately, the problem is that many of us were never taught to view the Bible as one cohesive story in the first place. We've been trained to think of the Bible more in light of its Table of Contents. For example, if someone asked you, "What is the Bible?" what would you say? I'm pretty sure the knee-jerk answer of most Christians would be, "The Word of God." A second question gets to the heart of the matter: "About what?"

8 What Is the Bible… Really?

One of the most interesting parts of being a teacher was witnessing how different students approached learning. Particularly how they approached different courses. In four decades, I saw the full spectrum. The overachiever, the apathetic, the clown, the 15-year-old pseudo-theologian. I was a Bible teacher, so I'd argue that the stakes were a little higher. We weren't engaging with AP Calculus or Chaucer, but the very Word of God. I've seen students break down and weep at the goodness of this good news. I've seen others have what I can only call "lizard eyes"—the blank stare that is a product of familiarity and coldness when it comes to spirituality, a frequent unintended consequence of Christian day school education. This was the hardest part of my job by far. Leaving seeds of truth on fallow soil—and then just waiting.

Though perspectives on the Bible are as varied as people themselves, I'd like to talk about three of them. And remember, if the One Story is the determining our life's plot, then how we view it is crucial.

The first way—a minority view—is what I call "The Bible as textbook." Some people of faith speak about the Bible objectively, as a sort of divine textbook that speaks to all of life—from psychology to ethics to science. They tend to emphasize its propositions, words, and content. The phrase "propositional truth" carries great currency. For them, the Bible is a kind of citadel containing God's Truth, so it needs to be preserved and defended at all costs. As a result, apologetics—the reasonable defense of the faith—is held up as a key weapon for Christians in the never-ending battle to protect and preserve this Truth from an endless onslaught. If you are a disciple, you must forge a distinctly biblical worldview. You believe your responsibility to God and the Bible is to study it, know it, and defend it. That's what you do with citadels. The larger unbelieving culture is then constantly scrutinized and judgment passed on all that is "unbiblical." The Scriptures are frequently cited to refute and rebuke improper thinking and conduct of those *outside* the faith. This tends to generate debate (and sometimes disparagement) when dealing with politics, abortion, marriage, parenting, gender identity, social justice, the environment, and so on. The emphasis here is on using the Bible's *content* as the standard for how to *think*. Developing a "Christian mind"—one able to discern which ideas, world views, and behaviors are true or false, right or wrong, good or bad—becomes the goal of Christian education. Scholarship and systematic theology are viewed as paramount. Orthodoxy equals total fealty to the Bible, and there are some strong feelings about denominational loyalty as well. (Recall, I have a seminary degree in this stuff. I'm not trying to discredit it.)

A second way to view the Bible—the majority view—is more personal. It's not so much a textbook as a *handbook*. A sort of "disciplopedia." A "go-to" for insights and principles for personal happiness and fulfillment in what is called "the Christian life." How to run a church, how to do ministry, how to manage a family, how to be financially secure. How to lose weight, how to have good sex. How to understand what God thinks about your Enneagram results. How to lead your dog to Christ. Well, maybe not that last one, but the list is endless. With the Bible as a disciplopedia, discipleship is understood in terms of Christian values and virtues. How a believer should be living and why. The emphasis is on a Christian lifestyle. Behaving like a Christian. The disciple's responsibility to the Bible is to study it, know it, and apply it. That's probably why there are a multitude of "Application Study Bibles" on the market. Different versions for girls, boys, students, adults, etc. Christian merchandising and marketing also have a firm foothold within this camp. At the end of the day, the Bible slowly becomes a source of divine guidance to help us live the life we've chosen for ourselves. We have a vague sense of spirituality because we are seeking His insights regarding *our* plans.

Now, to be fair, these previous two perspectives on the Bible are valid, and both have a place in the life of a believer. But, that place, I believe, is inside the circumference of this third view of the Bible. A third way to view the Bible—the neglected view—is as a *Story book*. Listen carefully. I don't mean a "storybook" like an anthology. Nearly half of our Bible consists of narratives of one type or another. But unlike a literary anthology, these stories are all related to (and part of) the same single, divine narrative for their ultimate meaning. A true metanarrative into which all human history fits and derives its meaning.

Of course, the Bible contains individual stories. But there's a beauty to those individual pieces that can only be seen when we step back and look at the big picture. Take, for example, the Book of Ruth. This love story centers around three characters: Naomi, her daughter-in-law "Ruth the Moabitess" (i.e., *not* a Jew), and an older man, Boaz. The story is full of intrigue, valor, suffering, and redemption—worthy of reading in its own right—but the Book of Ruth contains two priceless pieces of historical information that locate it in the One Story. The book opens in a manner worthy of a Tolkien epic: "In the time when the judges ruled . . ." This was a time of darkness in the history of the Jews, recorded in disgusting detail in the Book of Judges. The book closes with a ten-name genealogy that goes from Ruth's husband Boaz all the way backward to Judah (the forefather of the messianic line) and then forward to King David (who has yet to be born). What do we learn from this? Without Ruth, there is no King David. Turns out, she's King David's great-great-grandmother! And... she's not even a Jew! In fact, neither was her husband Boaz's mother. She was a Canaanite prostitute.

This is just one example of how a single story makes up the much larger Story. A thousand years later, Matthew will take this genealogy and weave it into an extended genealogy that points to Yeshua. This was the more significant reason for these names being listed in Ruth in the first place! It turns out Ruth was part of something much older, longer, and more magnificent than she could ever know. And that Story isn't over yet. This also means the Books of Judges and Ruth have *everything* to do with *our* lives. Not just theirs.

And here's the heavy part...exciting, but still...pretty heavy. My responsibility to this Story is to study it, know it, *and* submit to its storyline because I'm now in it. This is the true basis for what we summarily call discipleship...submitting to God's storyline. Theologian (and poet) Eugene Peterson so aptly summarizes the priority of this view of the Bible over the other two:

> We have grown up in a culture that urges us to take charge of our own lives. We are master knowledge, divert ourselves . . . whatever. But use? Well-meaning people tell us that the Christian gospel will put us in

> charge of life, will bring us happiness and bounty. So we go out and buy a Bible. We adapt, edit, sift, summarize. We then use whatever seems useful and apply it in our circumstances; however we see fit. We take charge of the Christian gospel, using it as a toolbox to repair our lives, or as a guidebook for getting what we want, or as an inspirational handbook to enliven a dull day. But, we aren't smart enough to do that; nor can we be trusted to do that. The Holy Spirit is writing us into the revelation, the story of salvation. We find ourselves in the story as followers of Jesus. Jesus calls us to follow him, and we obey—or we do not. This is an immense world of God's salvation that we are entering; we don't know enough to use or apply anything. Our task is to obey—believingly, trustingly obey. Simply obey in a "long obedience."[1]

The real tragedy, beloved, is that we haven't been taught to think in terms of God's Story, so we end up living in terms of our own. We look to the Bible for insight on how to best live out our own stories.

Remember what I said earlier when it comes to many passages of Scripture (the Old Testament in particular), we think of ourselves too little? And that's because we don't see ourselves as Story-dwellers and Story stewards. We think of the Bible as a list of stories to memorize rather than the single Story that has absorbed us. But we're part of it now. We're tasked with affirming, protecting, and telling it.

So as we conclude this chapter, let's recap. Like we talked about with the flipsides of the Story words, the Bible is also multidimensional, and we must also view it like a "spinning coin." The propositional, practical, and narrative views of the Bible all have their place, but I'm suggesting that the first two must be subservient to the third. When we lose sight of the One Story, we are left with a partial picture that quickly assumes the role of the whole picture. And as we have talked about since page one, when it comes to the One Story, half-truths are not truths at all. And half-truths taught as truths become the parents of more half-truths assumed to be true. Before long, you have an entire theology that seems logical but isn't biblical. And because we who are believers base our lives on our theology, this half-truth theology becomes the justification for a life that seems Christian but isn't. Getting the Story right isn't just important—it's vital. So, let's spend some time doing just that.

9 "Let's Work Our Way Backwards"

I want to open this chapter with a quiz that might help you understand just how much we've been conditioned to think of the Bible as an anthology rather than a single narrative. As I said, I was a teacher. At this point in my life, it's part of my DNA to give quizzes. Below I've reproduced a standard Table of Contents for the 39 Old Testament books of a Protestant Bible. (It goes left to right, top to bottom.) Assuming that Genesis is the beginning of the story, I'd like you to mentally draw a line after the book where you think the actual *storyline* of the Old Testament ends. In other words, the book after which history stops moving forward. Don't listen to the little voice inside you telling you to skip to the next paragraph. Just take the quiz.

> Genesis • Exodus • Leviticus • Numbers • Deuteronomy • Joshua
> Judges • Ruth • 1 Samuel • 2 Samuel • 1 Kings • 2 Kings • 1 Chronicles
> 2 Chronicles • Ezra • Nehemiah • Esther • Job • Psalms • Proverbs
> Ecclesiastes • Song of Solomon • Isaiah • Jeremiah • Lamentations
> Ezekiel • Daniel • Hosea • Joel • Amos • Obadiah • Jonah • Micah
> Nahum • Habakkuk • Zephaniah • Haggai • Zechariah • Malachi

So, where did you put your line? What is the span of books that comprises the entirety of Old Testament history? Did you think I was messing with you with that question? Just playing a trick? I wasn't. Most of the believers I've taught over the past 40 years have no idea that the first seventeen books on that list contain the entire flow of history of the Old Testament. And that the remaining 22 books all fit within the timeframe of those first seventeen. Twelve books of prophecy were written during the time of 2 Kings alone. In other words, the Old Testament story "ends" after Esther. (Actually, it ends after Nehemiah because Esther took place halfway through Ezra!)

The point of the quiz is that if the Bible is a narrative, we should read it that way. Going from "cover to cover" is one of the worst ways to read the Bible. You end up reading Zechariah second to last even though he ministered during the days of Ezra, 23 books earlier on the list. But we don't know this because we don't know the narrative. Let me show you what I mean.

Imagine that Revelation, the *end* of the Story, is the only book of the Bible we have to learn from. Let's start at the end and work our way backward. The final verse will leave you perplexed: "The grace of the Lord Jesus be with all. Amen."

Now, if this is all we've been given of the Bible, you are probably wondering who "Jesus" is. (His name appears over six hundred times in the four Gospels, but you don't have those.) You are also struck by the presence of "Lord" attached to his name. In first-century Rome, it was illegal to attribute "Lord" to anyone except the emperor.

You still don't know what this last sentence of the Bible means, but you keep going. Go backward five more verses, and you run into someone with the nickname "the root" who is a descendant of another person, "David." Again, no clue who David or this "root" are unless you go to the Books of Samuel, Ruth, 1 Chronicles, and Isaiah. But, as I said, you don't have them.

Moving "ahead" a little further, you hit a triad of weird, paired descriptors: "Alpha and Omega," "first and last," and "beginning and end," which are related. Your gut tells you they point to someone, but because there's no book of Isaiah for context, you're out of luck.

Then comes a "Lamb," whom you will discover has a lead role in Revelation because it appears twenty-nine times. This stumps you, too. If only you had John's Gospel and Peter's letters to discover that Lamb is Jesus.

Next, you run into a pair of similar phrases: the "book of life" and the "tree of life." But you don't have Genesis and Exodus to provide the meaning to both of those phrases. So you keep moving "forward," hitting a barrage of names, descriptions, and recurring ideas. If you are trying to piece together significance from this book alone (without the rest of the Bible as context), you will have no idea who and what is significant, but making a list might provide some threads:

- There's a "holy city" called Jerusalem.

- The number *twelve* seems important, appearing nine times in two chapters. There are twelve gates in this "holy city" and twelve foundation stones. Twelve individuals, known as "apostles," are associated with each of the foundation stones. And there are twelve tribes, one connected with each of the gates.
- These tribes are all descended from a man whose name sounds more like a city than a person. His name is "Israel."
- There is a character named Moses who is only mentioned once but is linked to "the Lamb," so perhaps he's significant.

Making sense of this is like standing with your nose to a single tile of a mosaic and trying to guess the image on the wall. But, if we pull back and look at the whole story containing an additional 65 books, we can draw countless insights from the "clues" listed above. Here are just a few of them that come to mind:

- This "holy city" (Jerusalem) is a popular place, appearing over 800 times in thirty-five other books of the Bible. It first appears as "Salem" in Genesis and "Jerusalem" in Joshua.
- In the Gospel of Mark, we learn what an "apostle" is and who the specific apostles were.
- The twelve tribes are explained in Genesis. So is "Israel," who used to be called "Jacob."
- Fifteen hundred years separate the names on the stones ("apostles") and the names on the gates (tribes).
- Moses (who made a quick cameo in Revelation) is actually a key character. He is mentioned nearly 900 times in thirty other books of the Bible. The first time he appears is in Exodus, a book written about 1,500 years *before* Revelation!
- And the Lamb who stars in Revelation we discover was foreshadowed in Genesis in the story of Abraham's testing and the first Passover in Exodus. The Lamb was also prophetically described in Isaiah and identified by John the Baptist in the Gospel of John.

So, what am I doing here? I'm trying to show that Revelation is incomprehensible apart from the rest of the Bible, *especially* the beginning. Not because of all the imagery and visions, but because of all the "normal" stuff. The names, the places, the metaphors. Why is this so important? Because it's the *end* of the

One Story and making sense of it requires knowing everything that preceded it. Sounds a little like a narrative to me. How about you?

The biblical writers thought and lived in light of a single storyline because they were part of it. John wrote Revelation at the same time he was writing another book—the Gospel of John. He began his Gospel with this phrase: "In the beginning . . ." This is no coincidence. The opening phrase of Genesis—the book that begins the Story—is the same! The parallel was intentional because John understood that this is One Story! In a profound sense, John was writing a continuation of Genesis, not just the fulfillment of prophecy.

In writing Revelation, the mystery and even the confusion of what John saw did not stop him from being awestruck and overwhelmed by it: "I, John, am the one who heard and saw these things. And when I heard and saw them, I fell down to worship at the feet of the angel who showed them to me."[1]

John's response was worship. And, as we'll see later, Paul did the same thing when he tried to express all that the One Story entailed. It's also what you and I are going to do at the end of the Story, too—fall on our faces and worship—we, and everything in heaven, on earth, and under the earth.[2]

Stuck in the Present

The idea that a single story can point back to the beginning of time and forward into an unknown eternity is somewhat mind-blowing for the modern individual. In Chapter 1, thanks to Bilbro, we learned that most of us are mired in the present time (*chronos*). Since we are *chronos*-focused, we stay on the hamster wheel of current events or what we like to call the "news."

Unlike the Navajos we mentioned earlier, we are disconnected from our spiritual history. We can't recount or retell the "origin story" of the gospel. We think the gospel began with Jesus, but it is *much* older than Jesus. Jesus is older than "Jesus," if you understand what happened in the Incarnation. For Protestants, our sense of the history of the gospel typically doesn't go much further back than the Reformation in the 16th century.

Why does this matter? Because His Story is *our* history! All of it, beloved. Not just the New Testament and the churches that emerged from it. Look at the Exodus. Here the newly-revealed God of Israel delivered a newly-identified people from slavery. It was spectacular. The most important redemptive event in the Old Testament. It marked the beginning of the *visible* fulfillment of a promise God made to a wandering Chaldean pagan named Abram 500 years earlier. Yahweh built this event into the Jewish religious and agricultural calendar as well as their hymnal so that it would be burned in their minds.[3] But what about us? The Exodus is one of the most definitive events in our *own* spiritual heritage. According to missiologist Christopher Wright, "The Exodus was not a movement from slavery to freedom, but from slavery to covenant. Redemption was for relationship with the redeemer, to serve his interests and his purposes in the world."[4]

Passover, the night of the Exodus, was Yahweh's means to guarantee that His covenant people would never forget their *corporate* history—especially their bondage and deliverance—because their own *personal* history and purpose were derived from it! (As a side note, the Jewish festival of Passover is in no way hostile or contradictory to Christian theology. Why we didn't adopt the whole celebration instead of the abbreviated bread and wine version has always puzzled me.) Over time, we have lost sight of (or neglected) the unbroken continuity of redemptive history. The narrative of Israel in the Old Testament, it turns out, is the indispensable prelude to the chapter of the One Story we find ourselves in right now!

And here's another enormous detail from the *end* of the Story that has somehow fallen out of our biblical suitcase along the way. In the book of Revelation, John makes it indisputably clear that the Story does *not* end in "heaven." It ends where it started—in a garden—*on earth!*

We'll unpack this in the coming chapters, but for now, we should just know that the idea of "spending eternity in heaven" is not true, and it's not in the Scriptures. That's *not* where the Story ends. Take a minute here if you need to. The One Story ends *after* the final resurrection, and at that time, we will all be on a "new *earth*" in resurrected bodies! Noah will be there, David, Isaiah, Mary Magdalene, Simon of Cyrene, the Ethiopian eunuch, Saint Francis, John Calvin, Charles Wesley, Henri Nouwen, Martin Luther King Jr., Mahalia Jackson, Brennan Manning, Carl Ellis, the "cloud of witnesses" listed in Hebrews 11. I'll be there too. Real people in real time and space from as far back as Eden, in the presence of God and each other. Getting this right is *huge!* It transforms what we are inviting people into when we share the gospel, and more importantly, it shapes how we live now and why. Paul made it clear that there is an unbroken cause-and-effect relationship between this life and the next:

Have nothing to do with irreverent, silly myths. Rather train yourself for godliness; for while bodily training is of some value, *godliness is of value in every way, as it holds promise for the present life and also for the life to come.* The saying is trustworthy and deserving of full acceptance. For to this end we toil and strive, because we have our hope set on the living God, who is the Savior of all people, especially of those who believe. (1 Timothy 4:7–10)

"Godliness" was a topic that Paul spoke of to two young pastors, Timothy and Titus,[5] because the *pursuit* of godliness was for all believers. They all needed to be taught what it was and how to cultivate it. Why? Because "it holds promise for…the life to come." That's why Paul wanted Timothy and Titus to know this. The modern idea that all Christians will have an identical eternal experience is not in the Bible. In fact, the Bible teaches the opposite! When Jesus taught on "storing up treasure in heaven," it was in contrast to hoarding it here.[6] And Jesus' Parable of the Talents ends with different "rewards" for varying efforts.[7] So if this is true, some folks have treasures, and some don't. Some folks get rewards; some folks don't.

Again, I know I'm walking in a minefield here again by suggesting that our "works" on earth have a bearing on what our eternity will be like as individuals. Just so we're on the same page, "works" don't determine *where* we spend eternity. Remember in Chapter 5, we learned that the flipside of righteousness is works, but because Christ *is* our righteousness, there is nothing we have left "undone." I cannot stress that enough! But if we look at the Bible, the eternal state for believers on the new earth is *not* equal. It's not "everyone gets a participation trophy." I think we've assumed (or been taught) that after judgment, we will all mosey into "heaven," find our mansion, then hit the golf course. But everyone won't get an equal slice of the eternal pie. Though I don't fully understand it, I know it doesn't work that way.

If you are a Christian, it makes a difference how you are living right now! Paul says our lives as believers will be "tested by fire," based on what we've done: "If anyone's work is burned up, he will suffer loss, though he himself will be saved, but only as through fire."[8] This doesn't leave much room for interpretation. True believers will all spend eternity with Jesus, but if I may extend Paul's metaphor, some of us are coming in smelling a bit like an ashtray. Again, reward is not our motivation. Our motivation is Christ. Look at thief who was crucified beside Jesus—he was saved in the final moments of his life—and all that mattered was being with Jesus after that. But we who know Christ *before* our dying hour have a purpose in this life with eternal ramifications. If we are true to the Scriptures, then we live knowing that when *chronos* time ends, our life doesn't. But what is done in *chronos*, mindful of *kairos*, lasts forever. It took me a long time to see this. After studying my Bible more carefully, I discovered that it was a dangerously popular and pervasive error.

Let me come back to where we started: We need to know, really know, the narrative of the Bible. Not so we have answers for skeptics, or advice for parenting, but because it's *our* narrative. It's not just a story we've chosen to believe. It's the Story we're *in*! I'm not shaming anyone here, beloved. What you're reading on these pages was absent from my own life and ministry for nearly 40 years! I am simply inviting you who profess Jesus to take stock of what it is that determines what matters in your life. In the case of "heaven," perhaps we have grown up with these half-truths as I talked about, but we aren't engaged enough with the Story to realize our missteps. So we go on thinking that "heaven" is our destiny and what we are living for. Not knowing that the new earth is *where* we'll be when we've finished the work were supposed to be *living* for. And if we don't have the *end* of the One Story straight, most likely we've got the rest of it messed up too—which means we've lost the plot.

That brings me to one final idea before we close this chapter. It's a biblical theme that has the momentum to move us all the way back to Genesis via every book between.

> And when the seven thunders had sounded, I was about to write, but I heard a voice from heaven saying, "Seal up what the seven thunders have said, and do not write it down." And the angel whom I saw standing on the sea and on the land raised his right hand to heaven and swore by him who lives forever and ever, who created heaven and what is in it, the earth and what is in it, and the sea and what is in it, that there would be no more delay, but that in the days of the trumpet call to be sounded by the seventh angel, the mystery [*mustērion*] of God would be fulfilled, just as he announced [*euaggelizō*] to his servants the prophets. (Revelation 10:4–7)

This passage from Revelation (the book that closes our One Story) uses two words that point us back to the beginning of the Story and give meaning to everything between. They are the words *mystery* and *announced*, *mustērion* and *euaggelizō* in Greek. (Don't get hung up on the Greek here, just try to use them as magnifiers of meaning.) *Euaggelizō* is a member of a word family from which we derive our English word *evangelism*, the proclamation or announcement of the "good news." In our New Testament, *euaggelizō* is synonymous with preaching, particularly the preaching of the "good news." John tells us that Yahweh had "preached" a "mystery" to the prophets, and obviously He had done so *prior* to the days of Jesus.

The combination of these two words at the *end* of the Story is very significant. Preachers often tell us that in the Bible a "mystery" is something that was hidden but has now been revealed. That's helpful, but only marginally, because while it reveals to us what the Greek word *means*, it fails to tell us what this "mystery" actually *is*. We need to know the mystery to get the story, and to do that, we'll need to look at the reeducation of a rabid rabbi, a brilliant Benjamite Jew from Tarsus named Saul—the greatest "mystery" writer in the Bible. And, it turns out, the poster child for seeing the enormity of the Story.

10 New Eyes, Not Better Glasses

The story leading up to the transformation of Saul was a big deal to Yahweh. (Just for context, Paul was "Saul" before his conversion, but for the sake of consistency, I'm going to call him Paul throughout.) Paul's transformation story is the only narrative in the Book of Acts that appears more than once. God seems to have gone out of His way to make sure that everyone understood not *that* it happened but *how*. The beheading of James, the stoning of Stephen, even the events of Pentecost all get one spot, but Paul's encounter with Yeshua on the road to Damascus is rehearsed three times in Acts. Once by the author (Luke), and twice more from Paul himself in defense of his ministry. Here's Luke's original account (which he received from Paul because he wasn't there when it happened):

> But Saul, still breathing threats and murder against the disciples of the Lord, went to the high priest and asked him for letters to the synagogues at Damascus, so that if he found any belonging to the Way, men or women, he might bring them bound to Jerusalem. Now as he went on his way, he approached Damascus, and suddenly a light from heaven shone around him. And falling to the ground he heard a voice saying to him, "Saul, Saul, why are you persecuting me?" And he said, "Who are you, Lord?" And he said, "I am Yeshua [Jesus], whom you are persecuting. But rise and enter the city, and you will be told what you are to do...Now there was a disciple at Damascus named Ananias. The Lord said to him

> in a vision, "Ananias." And he said, "Here I am, Lord." And the Lord said to him, "Rise and go to the street called Straight, and at the house of Judas look for a man of Tarsus named Saul…So Ananias departed and entered the house. And laying his hands on him he said, "Brother Saul, the Lord Jesus who appeared to you on the road by which you came has sent me so that you may regain your sight and be filled with the Holy Spirit." And immediately *something like scales fell from his eyes*, and he regained his sight. (Acts 9:1–6, 10–11, 17–18)

If we look at this narrative in terms of the One Story, we realize it must be critical to the Story if the Yahweh deemed it worth repeating three times. So, let's walk through this encounter carefully, starting with a simple fact: Paul never "became a Christian." To speak of his "conversion" is a misnomer. Paul didn't go from Jew to "Christian." For that matter, nobody "became a Christian" in Acts. Just as we said in the last chapter, there are miscalculations we carry with us as modern believers. Sometimes they result from our lack of really studying the Story.

But back to Paul. He was a Jew when he left Jerusalem, he was still a Jew when he was blind and shaken in Damascus, and he was *still* a Jew when he was under house arrest at the end of Acts. The man who "led him to Christ" was also a Jew, as were all the people he fellowshipped with over the days that followed.

Yet, if we venture further into the weeds, we must admit that Paul *was* a Jew, but in a sense, he also *wasn't*. He was the same person, radically changed. And the change was rooted in a total renovation of his understanding of the Hebrew Scriptures. Our thought of him "becoming a Christian" is an example of layering twentieth-century vocabulary (and context) over a first-century narrative. It's something we do all the time. When you hear the word *gospel*, if your mind goes comfortably to a *Four Spiritual Laws* gospel presentation, you're doing it again. What is called the "gospel" in our Bible, as we will discover, is inseparable from the One Story. And the Story, as we've seen just from looking at its *ending*, is a narrative that cannot be reduced to a PowerPoint slide gospel of "four points and a prayer."

When I first began to see the One Story for myself, I decided to track its presence in the life and teachings of Paul. In the process, I began to grasp just how radical Paul's transformation was. It made sense why he was so furious towards those who messed with "his gospel" and why he was so passionate about the temporary nature and purpose of Judaism. Although we have no record to substantiate it, I believe that shortly after this account in Acts, though he continued to frequent it, Paul never offered another *sacrifice* in the Temple in Jerusalem.

If we combine Luke's narrative account with Paul's two accounts, we get a fuller, albeit incomplete, version.[1] In Luke's opening, we are told that Paul was struck blind but "regained his sight" when Ananias laid hands on him. Ananias carried Yahweh's message, which included kings, Gentiles, Jews, and pain. Much attention is given to Paul's eyes. His story is the only account of literal blindness in Acts. However, there is a *second* reference to sight being restored in Acts, and it also involves Paul—but as the healer, not the one healed. This second reference provides insight into the intentional *manner* in which Paul's healing occurred.

Luke told us that "something like scales fell from his eyes" as he was restored to sight. We don't know whether Ananias is the one who saw them fall or if Paul *felt* them leave his eyes or both. But "scales" did fall. Why "scales?" No one ever experienced this kind of healing from Jesus. And more importantly, why *blindness*? Blindness and scales. Why not a vision and its illustration, like Peter on the roof in Joppa? Or an angelic appearance during prayer, like Cornelius experienced[2]?

I believe Paul answers that question seventeen chapters later. As a prisoner in Caesarea, he recounted the Damascus Road incident to King Herod Agrippa II. Here we get the expanded version of the story, especially more detail on just what Yahweh said to Paul that day:

> And when we had all fallen to the ground, I heard a voice saying to me in the Hebrew language, "Saul, Saul, why are you persecuting me? It is hard for you to kick against the goads." And I said, "Who are you, Lord?" And the Lord said, "I am Yeshua whom you are persecuting. But rise and stand upon your feet, *for I have appeared to you for this purpose*, to appoint you as a servant and witness to the things in which you have seen me and to those in which I will appear to you, delivering you from *your people and from the Gentiles—to whom I am sending you to open their eyes*, so that they may turn from darkness to light and from the power of Satan to God, that they may receive forgiveness of sins and a place among those who are sanctified by faith in me." (Acts 26:14–18)

The reference to "opening the eyes" of the Jews and Gentiles would have opened Paul's *spiritual* eyes, even while his physical eyes were glued shut. Paul, a dedicated Pharisee, would have done a mental search, hearing these words from Yeshua. He would have known that Yeshua was drawing directly from a messianic promise in Isaiah 42 that links the ministry of the Messiah with opening blind eyes and refers to the servant of Yahweh as being blind himself.[3] Without the *whole* picture, Paul's tiny world of Judaism suddenly wasn't big enough for God and His Story, which Paul (and the rest of the Jews) had assumed was exclusively theirs.

New Paul—Old Story

Immediately, the *purpose* of Judaism (as Paul knew it) was called into question. What he thought was the *whole* story turned out to be a mere "chapter" in a story much older than Abraham, much broader than the Jews, and more profound than law-keeping. That day on the road, Paul's personal, theological, and spiritual universe was beginning to be reordered. Perhaps a little like our experience early in this book, pushing our understanding of the Story words from two dimensions to four.

And although Luke's record includes very few details of this tectonic shift in Paul's outlook, the record of Paul's three missionary journeys, his arrest and imprisonment in Jerusalem and Caesarea, and his transport to Rome and imprisonment are rich with insight. They provide us with snapshots of his transformed theology, his constant warfare with orthodox Judaism, and the growing number of Gentiles within his audiences. But Acts also gives us a chronological framework, a timeline in which Paul wrote all but three of his letters. From his correspondence to the churches on the mainland of Asia, Macedonia, and Greece, we can extract even more pieces to the puzzle as he himself began to understand the One Story. And this sends us back to our clue factory—the Book of Revelation. The two words we highlighted in Revelation, *mustērion* and *euaggelizō*, it turns out, were already in the Story, thanks to Paul, who wrote about them thirty years before John penned Revelation.

The word "preach" is scattered throughout Paul's writings and those of Luke, his personal physician and traveling companion. Of the fifty-four appearances of "preach" in our New Testament, all but eight are from Luke and Paul. When it comes to the word "mystery," Paul is responsible for twenty of the twenty-seven occurrences in our New Testament. This idea of mystery is a big deal to Paul, just as it was to Yahweh. And *why* it's a big deal is no mystery for those who have had their scales (or "veil," if you prefer Paul's word for it) removed.[4] Mystery became the hat-rack for everything he learned about his new, infinitely-expanded Story. It was the genome of redemption. For Paul, everything came back to it and was derived from it.

Tracing the use of mystery in Paul's writings is informative but frustrating. Paul tells us that this mystery had been "hidden for *generations* and *ages*."[5] It's startling to discover that the people most likely to understand it—the authors—were precisely the ones who didn't "get it." Later on, Peter informs us that even the prophets had no idea what they were actually being inspired to write in terms of what we now know as "mystery."[6] He goes further and says that even the *angels* have to sit in the audience along with the rest of humanity and learn:

> Concerning this salvation, the prophets who prophesied about the grace that was to be yours searched and inquired carefully, inquiring what person or time the Spirit of Christ in them was indicating when he predicted the sufferings of Christ and the subsequent glories. It was revealed to them that they were serving not themselves but you, in the things that have now been announced to you through those who preached the good news to you by the Holy Spirit sent from heaven, *things into which angels long to look*. (1 Peter 1:10–12)

It gets better. Paul tells us that Yahweh's current intention is that *you and I* (i.e., the Church) are to be the broadcasters from which the hosts of heaven, hell, and humanity will gain a progressive understanding of this mystery that has been hidden for ages:

> To me, though I am the very least of all the saints, this grace was given, to preach to the Gentiles the unsearchable riches of Christ, and to bring to light for everyone what is the plan of the *mystery* hidden for ages in God who created all things, *so that through the church the manifold wisdom of God might now be made known to the rulers and authorities in the heavenly places.* This was according to the eternal purpose that he has realized in Christ Jesus our Lord. (Ephesians 3:8–11)

In this passage, we see Paul's gratitude for his calling and the message he has been stewarded to preach: the veil of the mystery has been lifted. In his Corinthian correspondence, Paul shares another snippet of how he came to further understand what had been hidden for eons from angels and archangels and for centuries from prophets and kings:

> I must go on boasting. Though there is nothing to be gained by it, I will

> go on to visions and revelations of the Lord. I know a man in Christ who fourteen years ago was caught up to the third heaven—whether in the body or out of the body I do not know, God knows. And I know that this man was caught up into paradise—whether in the body or out of the body I do not know, God knows—and he heard things that cannot be told, which man may not utter. On behalf of this man I will boast, but on my own behalf I will not boast, except of my weaknesses—though if I should wish to boast, I would not be a fool, for I would be speaking the truth; but I refrain from it, so that no one may think more of me than he sees in me or hears from me. (2 Corinthians 12:1–6)

The life-altering nature of that experience, paired with what he saw and learned, launched Paul on a trajectory that was destined to land him in trouble—not just with his fellow Jews but with Yahweh Himself. In short, what Paul experienced was so totally removed from the experience of any living person, including the twelve apostles up to now, Yahweh had to quarantine the inevitable ascent of arrogance. He did to him what He did to Jacob eighteen centuries earlier—He crippled him. Only Paul didn't come away from the experience with a limp. Yahweh gave him a thorn instead, a physical limitation whose very nature would remind him to be humble. We don't know what that thorn was. But it was severe, permanent, and not something he could "pray away."

> So to keep me from becoming conceited because of the surpassing greatness of the revelations, a thorn was given me in the flesh, a messenger of Satan to harass me, to keep me from becoming conceited. Three times I pleaded with the Lord about this, that it should leave me. But he said to me, "My grace is sufficient for you, for my power is made perfect in weakness." (2 Corinthians 12:7–9)

So Paul, like Noah, Abraham, Moses, and Jonah before him, joined the long line of chosen vessels who discovered that it's better to submit than to run. He accepted *both* the privilege of his transformation *and* the thorn that came with it. In exchange, he was given insight into "the mystery of Christ, which was not made known to the sons of men in other generations." For Paul, this mystery included Christ Himself, Christ and the church, the will, wisdom, and grace of God, and this new reality called "the gospel."[7] Paul also learned about the enormity of this mystery. It was conceived before time and it started with Adam, not Abraham. It included "all things, and all nations," not just Israel and the Jews.[8] And according to Paul, the "plan for the fullness of time," conceived and orchestrated in *kairos* time had finally arrived in *chronos* time, weaving the two together for the rest of the Story:

> …making known to us the mystery of his will, according to his purpose, which he set forth in Christ as *a plan for the fullness of time (kairos), to unite all things in him, things in heaven and things on earth.* (Ephesians 1:9–10)

But when *the fullness of time (chronos) had come*, God sent forth His Son, born of woman, born under the law, to redeem those who were under the law, so that we might receive adoption as sons.[9]

Yahweh's Hidden Highways

There must have been a hint of familiarity to the thoughts ricocheting in Paul's head after his encounter with Yeshua that day on the road. A "storied" universe, characterized by a layered revelation available to some and hidden from others, was not new to him. It was part of the fabric of the Jewish Scriptures. What Paul labels a "mystery" in his own writings had been Yahweh's *modus operandi* since the beginning. Repeatedly in the Jewish Scriptures, God separated His "ways" and His "thoughts" from His "acts," and who was and was not privy to each. Digging a little further into the Story, it's obvious His "ways" are a reference to His plans rooted in the grander reality He is directing in *kairos* time. There is a clear indication of intention, progress, and purpose to these "ways" of Yahweh. A trajectory of purpose. A plot, a narrative of sorts.

This being the case, the pleading of Moses to the Lord, "Now therefore, if I found favor in your sight, please show me now your ways, that I may know you in order to find favor in your sight,"[10] must be understood as his desire to understand just what Yahweh was doing. We see this same sense of a "storied reality" even in the Psalms: "He made known his ways to Moses, his acts to the people of Israel."[11] The psalmist separates God's "ways" from His "acts," the former apparently "classified," and the latter public.

Evidently, Moses was granted "clearance" from Yahweh, so he had access to a hidden understanding of what God was doing, i.e., these "ways." From elsewhere in the Bible, we know that Yahweh considered Moses a friend.[12] So Moses is granted a brief and privileged glance at a fragment of a bigger picture—the One Story. And in the process, he comes to realize that his own destiny is now inseparable from its plot. Paul would make the same discovery 1,400 years later!

It's Isaiah, however, who educates us regarding the profoundly divine nature of the One Story, and why Paul needed to be "caught up into the third heaven" to comprehend it.

> For my thoughts are not your thoughts,
> neither are your ways my ways, declares the LORD.
> For as the heavens are higher than the earth,
> so are my ways higher than your ways
> and my thoughts than your thoughts.
> "For as the rain and the snow come down from heaven
> and do not return there but water the earth,
> making it bring forth and sprout,
> giving seed to the sower and bread to the eater,
> so shall my word be that goes out from my mouth;
> it shall not return to me empty,
> but it shall accomplish that which I purpose,
> and shall succeed in the thing for which I sent it."
> (Isaiah 55:8–11)

Yahweh's "ways" and "thoughts" are categorically different from ours. They are also "higher" than ours and beyond our power to comprehend. We reason and conclude in an infinitely inferior way. Again, there is this notion of the "ways" of God being far removed, not only from our understanding, but our ability to recognize them around us. Even the Bible can't help here, as if we merely needed the Scriptures to help us understand some deep idea. The humbling truth is that there is something at work here, a grand drama that is sovereignly unfolding beyond our sensibilities. And, for the present, Moses, Isaiah, and a long line of faithful people up to John the Baptizer are given an appetizer and told that the main course will not be served in their lifetime. His "ways" are the truth, the whole truth, and nothing but the truth.

Unfortunately, no one could handle the truth . . . *then*.

Jesus also alludes to the reality of *kairos* at the Last Supper. He announces an enormous status update for his apostles: "No longer do I call you servants, for the servant does not know what his master is doing; but I have called you friends, for all that I have heard from my Father I have made known to you."[13] At the time, they had experienced private explanations of parables, teaching around campfires and in homes during his three years of ministry, and several V.I.P. experiences such as the transfiguration and the Garden of Gethsemane. But unbeknownst to them, friendship with Jesus would soon include insider information regarding Yahweh's "plan for the fullness of time." The One Story would reset the trajectory of their lives and the cause of their deaths.

Even Paul was never entirely comfortable with his understanding of this mystery's breadth and length and height and depth. This notion that God's "ways" are removed from our grasp was evident in Paul's grappling with Yahweh's purposes for His "chosen people" in Romans 9–11. Much of Paul's commentary in this portion of the book has to do with the difference between national and spiritual Israel. Not having all the answers pushes Paul not to despair but to praise: "O the depths of the riches, and the wisdom, and the knowledge of God! How unsearchable are his judgments, how inscrutable his ways!"[14]

Tragically, these chapters have at times been reduced to a theological meth lab to cook the doctrine of election. If we take Paul's words out of context, we won't see them as a spell-binding synopsis of some key players in this mysterious One Story. Even though he didn't have the whole picture, Paul got the point. He was grateful to have a few crumbs of understanding from the table of God's ways. That's why he ends his discussion of the purpose of God's elective plans for Israel *on his knees*, not sitting or standing.

But Paul didn't stay on his knees. The new eyes (and the thorn that accompanied them) began working in tandem. This man who had tried to extinguish the spark that had appeared among his own people discovered he had caught fire, and the flame now consumed him. And like the bush that attracted Moses, Paul would become a light to the Gentiles — the very thing the children of Abraham were supposed to have done all along.

11 The Power of the Gospel: Narrative or Imperative?

During an emotional seaside farewell, Paul told a group of elders from Ephesus, "I do not account my life of any value nor as precious to myself, if only I may finish my course and the ministry that I received from the Lord Jesus, to testify to the gospel of the grace of God."[1]

Paul made this comment a decade before his death. He did not know that finishing the race and keeping the faith would also entail the loss of this life he counted of so little value in comparison with his place in the Story. I believe Paul finally clearly saw the connection between *who* he was (which he so richly explains in his letters) and this "mystery" of which he was given privileged access. His own purpose became defined and driven by it. The torn veil of Jerusalem's Temple on Good Friday was not just a symbol. It was the beginning of the end of mystery.[2] And Paul was the herald of *that* "good news."

Paul and the early church had a name for this death and resurrection of understanding, this unveiled "mystery." They called it the "gospel." And again, it *wasn't* four points and a prayer. It was the One Story of the One God, a plan for the fullness of time to unite all things in heaven and on earth in Christ. And most importantly, according to Paul, this didn't begin in a manger outside the holy city. It began in a tent somewhere on a journey from Ur to Canaan. It was something that Yahweh "pre-preached" to Abraham: "And the Scripture, foreseeing that God would justify the Gentiles by faith, preached the gospel beforehand to Abraham, saying, 'In you shall all the nations be blessed.'"[3]

If you look at Yahweh's invitation to Abram in Genesis 12 carefully, you'll see clearly that it was personal, parochial, global, and missional in nature. It was for Abram, his descendants, the nations, and ultimately for Yahweh Himself. Reading that encounter through new eyes with scales removed makes those few verses explode with meaning. *This* is what captured Paul on the road that day and consumed him for the rest of his life. His Jewish pedigree was suddenly less meaningful. In a status-driven culture, the only thing that now mattered was his new status as an adopted son in the household of Yahweh.[4]

Luke informs us that Paul had previously been energized by threatening and slaughtering Christians,[5] but the intensity of his fury was not quelled after his transformation. It was redirected. Paul's emotion and resolve spilled over into his ministry, both to the recipients of grace *and* its opponents. We read about his tireless and selfless service to the One for Whom he was a *doulos*, a bondservant. This service was always to draw people *into* the Story of the mystery hidden for ages and then equip them to do the same for others.[6]

> Him we proclaim, warning everyone and teaching everyone with all wisdom, that we may present everyone mature in Christ. For this I toil, struggling with all his energy that he powerfully works within me. (Colossians 1:28–29)

For Paul, to "mature in Christ" had to do with transformation. The increasingly visible presence of the risen Christ in the lives of those whose sins are forgiven was to be the new norm. In a comment to the believers of Galatia, he lamented how he was in the "anguish of childbirth until Christ be formed in you!"[7] And what he anguished over in *their* lives, he did for himself, too.

> I have been crucified with Christ. It is no longer I who live, but Christ who lives in me. And the life I now live in the flesh I live by faith in the Son of God, who loved me and gave himself for me. (Galatians 2:20)

It is impossible to inherit Abraham's *blessing* and not inherit his *mission* with it. We did not include this in the "flipsides" of part one, but in a very real sense, the flipside of blessing is mission. This good news, the unfolding of this mystery, this plan for the fullness of time, this One Story of the One God is *not* like a beautiful photograph or even a wonderful film that we want people to notice. It's not even like the story of your own conversion, a past event with present implications and future promise. The One Story of the Bible *isn't* over. Easter Sunday is the centerpiece of the Story and makes sense of everything that led up to that grueling weekend. But the crucifixion marked the curse of Eden beginning to work its way backward. Everything now flows *from* the Cross. Grace is always in motion. Like manna in the Old Testament, grace putrefies when hoarded by individuals, churches, or systematic theologies. The Story isn't something to point people *back* to. It's something to draw people *into*.

When asked about evangelism, I often share a simple analogy. Contrary to popular belief, Christians are not casting life preservers from the bank to people in a river. They're not rescuing the drowning by dragging them to safety. No, it's more like throwing a rope to people on the bank, pulling them *into* the raging torrent of grace with us.

As I said in the opening, the One Story isn't easy to swallow. This is no tale for cowards or narcissists. Annie Dillard, in her inimitable style, paints an intriguing and lucid portrait of this Book that *is* The Story:

> This Bible, this ubiquitous, persistent black chunk of a bestseller, is a chink—often the only chink—through which winds howl. It is a singularity, a black hole into which our rich and multiple world strays and vanishes. We crack open its pages at our peril. Many educated, urbane, and flourishing experts in every aspect of business, culture, and science have felt pulled by this anachronistic, semi-barbaric mass of antique laws and fabulous tales from far away; they entered its queer, straight gates and were lost. Eyes open, heads high, in full possession of their critical minds, they obeyed the high, inaudible whistle, and let the gates close behind them.[8]

Getting this single-story perspective on the Bible radically transforms how we talk about the Bible. If this Story is real, and it is true, *and* it is God's Story and not my own creation, it should elicit a heart of worship in us for its complexity and enormity. In Romans, Paul cranks on for 16 chapters about deep theology and its profound implications for the world's most influential city. Then, as he wraps it all up, he lays this card on the table. (Note his use of many of the words we've looked at):

> Now to him who is able to strengthen you according to my *gospel* and the *preaching* of Jesus Christ, according to the revelation of the *mystery* that was kept *secret* for long ages but has now been disclosed and through the prophetic writings has been made known to all *nations*, according to the

command of the eternal God, to bring about the obedience of faith—
to the only wise God be glory forevermore through Jesus Christ! Amen.
(Romans 16:25–27)

This is the worship that results from seeing the Story of God for what it is. Paul saw it. And it captured him. We need to let it capture us.

And getting all this right should also make submitting ourselves to God a reasonable thing. What do I mean? Well, this idea that God has a metanarrative, "a plan for the fullness of time," radically informs and transforms what it means to be a disciple. A Christ-follower. It means that the Bible's authority is *not* the authority of command. It is not imperative. The Bible is *not* a book of "thou shalts" and "thou shalt nots." It's *not* a book of rules and restrictions which are the authority of *imperative*. If you've viewed the Bible this way, I want to ask you to have a funeral for that perspective. It's oppressive and produces people who are either angry, bitter, and resentful, or angry, mean, and arrogant. Or simply cynical.

On the other hand, if the Bible is the Story of God, its authority is the authority of *narrative*. A narrative, by virtue of what it is, has an authority built into the genre. The storyline has to be followed.

Let me show you what I mean. Imagine you and some friends are having a movie night. You're watching *The Social Dilemma* and right in the middle of one of the interviews with Tristan Harris, there's a ten-second blip from *Despicable Me 3*. What would you do? You'd look at each other and say, "What the heck! Why was that in there?"

That tug of confusion and even outrage is the point I'm trying to make. That's the *authority* of narrative. The nature of narrative prohibits inserting something (or someone) that doesn't belong in the storyline. This, beloved, is why submission to God—acknowledging His Lordship—is a reasonable response in the heart of anyone who is truly a Christ-follower. Suddenly, Lordship or discipleship no longer centers around obeying certain rules or even mastering certain spiritual disciplines like Bible reading, prayer, etc. Even though these are beneficial and important for spiritual vitality. If the Bible is truly God's narrative, God's Story, God's plan for the fullness of time to unite all things in heaven and in earth in Christ, then *my* calling is to submit to *that* Story. It means—and I want to say this humbly and gently—a believer makes every effort to find his or her place in God's Story, instead of trying to squeeze God into their own.

And do you know why? Because we're already in it!

So let's bring this section in for a landing. I know we've gotten slightly more existential in these chapters, but as I said, we'll keep wading out until we're in the deep end. I've thrown a lot at you, so let's retrace our steps. If you don't remember anything, try to remember this: Human beings are hardwired for meaning. Story (narrative) brings meaning. This is not a Christian thing. We've seen this in cultures since the earliest record of human existence. We are going to have a story, even if we decide it's the *absence* of a story (enter the "no-plot" peeps). Part of why we long for a story is in our very make-up. We were made in the image of the Master Storyteller who has given us not a textbook or a handbook or rulebook but a *narrative*. His. The fact that the Bible is a narrative (and not an imperative) tells us not only what kind of Lord we serve but what kind of relationship He wants with us.

But narratives, while innate in us, are under attack. Deep engagement is under attack. The fact that you are even trying to read this book shows that you are willing to battle against the tech-shaped culture that feeds off our modern need for quick answers. All this plays into where we are today. Not knowing our own story. And because of that, we're getting a lot of things wrong. This can come from inaccurate teaching, but I'd argue it also comes from the fact that people don't realize we need the *entire* Story. As we saw while unpacking Revelation, if we just focus on parts of the One Story, we're left intrigued but confused. We have a few beautiful pieces of broken glass but no idea that it belongs to a mosaic that transcends present past and future — *kairos* and *chronos* time.

Narrative has authority. Like the intruding movie example, we feel it when the rules are broken. We won't stand for what shouldn't be there. That is the power of narrative's authority, and that's why we, as believers, will feel called to submit to Gods' storyline once we really see it. We've seen what happens when you don't do that. We started with Solomon's unquenchable quest for plot, and we spent a lot of time with Paul who was both satiated *and* mystified once he realized the depth of the Story. Like the rest of us, he was limited by the "mysteries" of this text, but he got the importance of the oneness of it. The Jewish part of him understood the continuity. That this thing reaches all the way back to God's promise to Abraham, thanks to Moses who wrote those Jewish Scriptures that Paul (a diligent Jew) had likely memorized. But here's the kicker. The Story wasn't just for him (personal) and the Jews (parochial), it was for the Gentiles (global) and God himself. Paul saw it in 4D and had a thorn in the flesh to prove it! The Story was enough. Enough for Paul to die for it and the Gentiles Yahweh had called him (and us) to bring into it.

This narrative is as enormous as it is mysterious, beloved. I hope, in my profusion of cross-referencing, that I have not discouraged you but birthed a hunger to know it and step more fully into it. So, let's do just that.

PART

The One Story of the One God

12 ACTS I – III: Commencement, Conflict, Complication

"In the Beginning . . ."

Okay, it's finally time to tell you a story. *The Story.* It's a good one—it's long—but as I've promised you, if you get this Story right, it will become the key to living in *chronos* time, with your heart rooted in *kairos*. And the more time you spend *with* it, the more you will want to be *in* it.

A few chapters back, I suggested that reading the Bible in blind chronological fashion has some challenges, so as we break down this One Story in the following chapters, we're going to do so in a hybrid manner. We'll follow the table of contents (Genesis to Revelation), but we will also pull up to 100,000 feet, tracking the single Story within a linear path. I want you to start thinking of the Bible as one long drama comprised of five acts. So let's start at the beginning when the curtain first opens on a backdrop of thick, black nothingness.

ACT I— Commencement (Genesis 1–2)

Like any good narrative, our story begins with an introduction. A stage is set, key characters make initial appearances, and a relational context is established, helping us connect the "who" and the "where." The majestic account of Creation in Genesis 1 catapults us from telescopic (the entire universe) to microscopic (an idyllic garden called Eden). We are introduced to a couple (Adam and Eve) installed by God as co-regents, ruling on His behalf over all He had made. God charged them to "be fruitful and multiply" and "fill the earth and subdue it."

They were to expand their influence beyond the Garden as image-bearers of God Himself. They were, in a sense, to "Edenify" the rest of creation.

In the words of one scholar, this was God's "Creation Project.[1] It was a peaceful arrangement. Everything that breathed was given everything that didn't breathe as food. God was pleased with all He had done, christening it "very good." Genesis 2 is a divine soliloquy, expanding our introduction to Adam whose name in Hebrew reflects humanity's place at the top of creation.[2] Things are as they're supposed to be.

Of course, we are all too familiar with this story. Most of us have heard it since childhood, but the Creation story is actually a *prequel* to the story of a "chosen people," and these people will be crucial in the rest of the Story. The formation of this distinct group begins with the birth of Moses in the second book, Exodus. That means the first audience of this narrative was the Jews newly freed from enslavement in Egypt. They would have been spellbound as they listened to Moses recount the Creation tale. It was unlike anything they would have heard during those four centuries in Egypt. Beauty, wonder, and grace—the antithesis of creation accounts in the ancient Near East. No blood, no deific sex, no violence. A world in which everything flourished because all creation was doing exactly what it was designed to do. It was a world characterized by purpose and endowed with fulfillment. And yet, as they listened, they must have wondered how a place of beauty and perfect peace—shalom—had been replaced with hatred, mistrust, and brutality that characterized their lives in slavery.

And as they followed along in Moses' account, they would find out. Enter the serpent.

ACT II—Conflict (Genesis 3–11)

According to Genesis 3, the serpent was "more crafty than any other beast of the field the Lord God has made." As the plot unfolds, we can see what makes him so. The serpent hijacks the Creation Project, "Edenifying" the world outside the Garden with evil instead of good. His strategy was masterful. If you read the account carefully, you'll discover that his work with Eve was finished long before she ate the fruit. The serpent turned Eve's focus from what she *had* to what she *did not* have. Adam and Eve were given the freedom to eat from every tree in the Garden—*every* tree—except one. God had *His* tree that they were to tend. Caring for it, while not eating from it, was their only assignment with a restriction. The serpent got Eve to focus on that single tree. Once he did that, it was game over. He had finished his work before her hand ever reached for the fruit.

The serpent really was the craftiest thing in the Garden. He still is.

That little "turn your gaze from what you have to what you don't" ploy sounds familiar, doesn't it? *Crafty* isn't a synonym for *creative*, but it is synonymous with *effective*. And when it comes to our Enemy, that's all that matters. In the chapters that follow, we will walk deep into the theological forest of what emerged in the Garden. We will find much more than two naked people evicted from paradise.

Here, to see how the universe tilted that day, let's return to our first Story word—sin. It's the word we always associate with guilt, that embarrassed covering of our "nakedness." But as we saw earlier, its flipside reveals much more than that. It is the *corruption* of everything good, and it started right at that moment. Like in a Disney movie, the dark shadow spread from the Garden, leaving no element of humanity untouched. Remember the "former things"—the death, the pain, the outcry…the loss of shalom? Those are the ripple effects of that one choice. Things are no longer as they are supposed to be. If we look at it in narrative terms, this was the introduction of "the conflict," and even as I am writing this, it is not resolved fully—yet.

But back to the Story. After a global flood recounted in Genesis 6 through 9, God gave Noah and his sons a second chance to fulfill the Edenic command: "Be fruitful and multiply, fill the earth and subdue it." But it's as though the seeds of failure are inherent in this second attempt because God adds a caveat to His charge. Capital punishment for capital murder is the new normal. Why? Because humanity bears the *imago Dei*, the image of God.[3] The *imago Dei* is the signature of God imprinted on us. We introduced this concept a few chapters back in talking about why we need design and plot—purpose. *Imago Dei* shows up in other places as well. We bear other marks of our Creator, like our need for justice, hence this shift to capital punishment.

For Moses' immediate audience, this "conflict" introduced in the Garden explained a lot. It helped them understand how their lives could have been marked with such pain and suffering in Egypt. But then, after nine chapters of dark narrative, the Author of the Story graciously provided some relief in the form of a protagonist—Abram of Ur.

This Abram will be mentioned nearly three hundred times in the Story, in slightly fewer than half of the books of our Bible. But to Moses' audience (who didn't have the whole story), Abram seemed like a wandering pagan. At least for a while.

ACT III — Complication (Genesis 12 – Malachi 4)

Okay, as promised, here's where we jump the linear train. This narrative is masterful, and the more we pour over it, the more it reveals itself to us in complexity. But that requires us to put some effort into approaching it, not just plowing through it in a Read-the-Bible-in-One-Year fashion. That's a valiant effort, and I'm not knocking it, but I'm not sure what kind of insight it will yield.

As we learned from the "pop quiz" a few chapters back, the portion of the Story that is in our Old Testament concludes with Nehemiah. Don't forget that twelve of the prophets lived and wrote during the time recorded in 2 Kings. That means that the twenty-two books that follow Nehemiah in the standard Bible should be read as supplemental—not sequential—material in the first three Acts of the Story. Understanding the *arrangement* of the books of our Bible can't be overstated when it comes to following the Story itself.

While we're on this thread, another helpful contextual note has to do with the notion of a *Jew*. In the Narrative section, we saw that Jewish identity played a key role in Paul's conversion story. But *Jew* has no meaning in the world of Adam. At this point of the Story, *Jew* is a theological construct in the mind of Yahweh, nothing more. Grasping this is vital because, although the first audience of Genesis had no *national* identity, they did have a very defined *racial* identity. They were a people distinct from the Egyptians. But that was not always the case. The remaining thirty-nine chapters of Genesis (the early developments of ACT III) provide the newly emancipated Hebrews with an answer to *who* they were and *why* they existed—their *identity* and *purpose*. This part of their "backstory" opened with a fuzzy statement of their *mission* as well. It was all there, easily visible to us in hindsight but not to them at the time. It's revealed in what theologians refer to as the "call" of Abram:

> Now the LORD said to Abram, "Go from your country and your kindred and your father's house to the land that I will show you. And I will make of you a great nation, and I will bless you and make your name great, so that you will be a blessing. I will bless those who bless you, and him who dishonors you I will curse, and in you all the families of the earth shall be blessed." (Genesis 12:1–3)

With these words, Yahweh introduced the plot—His "plan for the fullness of time (*kairos* time)" to turn the disaster of Eden backward. For the first time, we got a promise that will echo throughout the Story—the "blessing of the *goyim*" (the nations) through an elect people. What had been in the mind and heart of Yahweh since eternity past took on flesh in the person of Abram.

It's also significant (but easily overlooked) that Yahweh's "call" to Abram included the first appearance of the four-dimensional theology we labored to unpack in the first part of this book. Namely, that the personal (Abram) and parochial ("great nation") are perfected by the global ("all the families of the earth") and missional ("I will show, make, bless," etc.). Do you see that? All four dimensions were present in the very beginning. But unfortunately, as the Story unfolded, God's people tended to cherish the front side and forget the flipside. But let's keep moving.

What I call the "Complication" of Act III went on for nearly forty more books, increasing in complexity and depth. The Author gave some characters—Isaac, Jacob, and Judah—central roles. Others—Lot, Ishmael, and Esau, to name a few—got smaller roles. Joseph occupied more narrative real estate than anyone else in Genesis, yet he was reduced to bones carried out of Egypt and buried a few chapters later. The significance of Joseph's life might be perplexing until we remember that Moses' audience, as recent refugees from Egypt, would have soaked up every word. Joseph was the reason they were in Egypt for ten generations! They *needed* to know about Joseph, though *we* know that Judah, a supporting actor in Act III, would actually become the one son of Jacob who would carry the Story to completion.

Act III also contains the most significant event in the Old Testament and maybe one of the top three in the Story itself: the Exodus. Many of us falsely assume the departure of the Jews from Egypt was deliverance from bondage to freedom. But this is another error that leads us to miss the significance in our modern lives.

The Exodus was *not* deliverance from bondage to *freedom*. It was a deliverance from bondage to *covenant*, a different type of submission. The liturgical, agricultural, and civic calendars of the Jews were centered around this event. They still are. Understanding what was in the mind of Yahweh before and after this event is essential. If we derail here, we, as modern Abrahamic believers[4], miss the rest of the story and our place within it.

Yahweh's election of Israel was *purposeful* and corporate, not just providentially selective. Once He got them out of Egypt, He needed to get Egypt out of them. Hence, a host of laws making them distinct among the nations. His purpose for them had to do with their role in the Story, not their ease and retirement in Canaan. Yes, Yahweh took the Jews out of Egypt, but He brought them to Mt. Sinai, *not* Club Med. The Exodus cannot be separated from the "call" of Abram and the "blessing" of the nations four hundred thirty years earlier:

> Say therefore to the people of Israel, "I am the LORD, and I will bring you out from under the burdens of the Egyptians, and I will deliver you from slavery to them, and I will redeem you with an outstretched arm and with great acts of judgment. I will take you to be my people, and I will be your God, and you shall know that I am the LORD your God, who has brought you out from under the burdens of the Egyptians. I will bring you into the land that I swore to give to Abraham, to Isaac, and to Jacob. I will give it to you for a possession. I am the LORD." (Exodus 6:6–8)

They existed for the mission of Abraham, their father. Unfortunately, as I alluded to a few pages back, "election" would become the distorted grounds for *failing* in that mission rather than fulfilling it, as the remainder of Act III will bear out.

From the Exodus to the end of Act III, the plot thickens. Philistines, Hittites, Assyrians, and Babylonians made excursions into the world of the Jews, most of them unpleasant. Nations rise and fall. Major and minor characters came across the stage: Joshua, Ruth, Samuel, David, Ahab and Josiah, to name a few. But as the record reveals, these stewards of the Story of "blessing" were more a reflection of their culture than the God who called them *out* of it. A danger that has never quit hunting the people of God, even to this day.

As a result, a new role in the Story is needed, that of the *navi*, the "prophet." Individuals who spoke on behalf of Yahweh had periodically appeared in the Story, but this was different. Each time as God's chosen people began to chart their *own* adventure, He raised up men (nearly twenty of them) in rapid succession to speak to the kings appointed to lead His covenant people. The job of a Jewish king was to maintain righteousness and justice in the kingdom. The job of the prophet was to provide the king with a real-time evaluation of his performance. So, in the Story, prophets played a more vital role than kings.

Our failure or refusal to understand the role of the prophets has led to some theological imbalance. Prophets in the Bible are typically sorted into groups based on when they lived, whether they wrote or just spoke, who their audience was, and several other factors. But for our purposes, we will categorize them by their messages. There are essentially only two types of prophecies in our Story.

The first is what we might call "prescriptive" prophecy, messages that tell people how to live. Some call this "forth-telling." Prescriptive prophecy makes up most of our Bible. It deals with *their* present, not *our* future. This is a surprise to many modern believers, who've been conditioned to equate the word *prophecy* with the "end times." But once we begin to see them in relation to the kings rather than the people, our understanding changes.

I like to think of prophets who deliver these messages as confronting the "traitors." Whether it was naive stupidity (Hezekiah providing classified information to the Assyrians), or blatant idolatry and perversion (Ahab and Jezebel), prophets were primarily dispatched to address the sins of kings.[5] It is this type of prophecy that speaks loudest into our day if we give it a voice: "For my people have committed two evils: they have forsaken me, the fountain of living waters, and hewed out cisterns for themselves, broken cisterns that can hold no water."[6]

The second type of prophetic message is less frequent yet more popular among modern believers. It is called "predictive" prophecy, or "foretelling." Predictive prophecy was always about the future. The messages were often enshrouded in imagery and allusion, and thus they provide fruitful fodder for unscrupulous or impetuous pastors of today. "Bible prophecy" can act as Christian astrology, a quest for secret knowledge and the power that results from insider information. Knowing what others don't, or speaking with certainty about future events, creates a sort of gnostic aristocracy. Christian publishers and filmmakers have had a heyday exploiting this illicit marriage of plot hunger and our Adamic residue. When I was younger, a book was released taunting the notion that the UPC bar code system could be the mark of the Beast.[7] I still have a copy of *88 Reasons Why the Rapture Will Be in 1988* sitting on my bookshelf. I suspected it might be a collector's item someday, so I kept it.

But if predictive prophecy is not for hit movies and televangelists, then what's it for? Fortunately for us, the apostle Peter anticipated that question in the first century:

> But do not overlook this one fact, beloved, that with the Lord one day is as a thousand years, and a thousand years as one day. The Lord is not slow to fulfill his promise as some count slowness, but is patient toward you, not wishing that any should perish, but that all should reach repentance.

> But the day of the Lord will come like a thief, and then the heavens will pass away with a roar, and the heavenly bodies will be burned up and dissolved, and the earth and the works that are done on it will be exposed. *Since all these things are thus to be dissolved, what sort of people ought you to be in lives of holiness and godliness, waiting for and hastening the coming of the day of God,* because of which the heavens will be set on fire and dissolved, and the heavenly bodies will melt as they burn! But according to his promise we are waiting for new heavens and a new earth in which righteousness dwells. *Therefore, beloved, since you are waiting for these, be diligent to be found by him without spot or blemish, and at peace.* (2 Peter 3:8–14)

Peter informed his readers (and us twenty centuries later) that predictive prophecy's purpose was to serve as "trailers" for the Story. Yahweh gave His people periodic snapshots *of the future* to incevntivize them to live as Story-dwellers *in the present.* He gave glimpses of future scenes and the *end* of the Story so that there may be hope and strength *during* the Story — especially for our role in it. And just like prescriptive prophecy, predictive prophecy is primarily for the *present*, not the future. And this is as true for us in the 21st century as it was for God's people 800 years before Yeshua.

Every time Jesus was asked about the "last days," his first response was to warn about being misled in the present.[8] Even at the ascension, when the apostles were still anxious about the "end times," Jesus immediately drew them back to their purpose in the Story. He basically told them that it's none of their business when the Kingdom is coming in fullness.[9] This is similar to what Jesus told Peter when he was wondering what Jesus had in mind for John's future.[10] It was almost as if Jesus had said, "You're going to be crucified upside down in Rome, and John's going to die of old age on a Mediterranean island with a five-book contract. Do you have a problem with that, Peter?" Two different men. Two different roles. One Story.

So prophecy is a big part of Act III, and to interpret it properly, we must understand its role. Prophecy serves and exists for the Story. It has no purpose outside it. Biblical prophecy either addresses the "traitors" or provides the "trailers." But again, in *both* cases, its intended purpose influences the *present*, not the future. If we only think futuristically about biblical prophecy, we've gotten it wrong. And since prophecy comprises about one out of every three words of the Bible, we've gotten a lot of the Story wrong.

The Adamic residue in our human nature will always struggle with role envy, not just plot rejection. Isn't that what got Adam in trouble in the first place? Understanding this is especially relevant for us today when we are tempted to compare our place in the Story to others. The Bible has a word for acceptance of one's role in the Story. It's called *contentment*. Paul said it was a secret he had learned.[11] But then again, if there was ever someone who *knew* his place in the Story, it was Paul.

Okay, enough of the aside, let's get back to tracking the Story. Genesis 12 through Malachi (Act III) turns out to be very long, spanning some 1,500 years. It starts with the introduction of Abram, a solitary and migratory figure, and it ends with the return of a kingless nation to the ruins of Jerusalem. Yahweh brought forth nations and kings from the loins of Abraham, as He had promised, but the flames of those hopes dwindled to smoldering ash. In only four centuries, Israel declined, going from a glorious, expansive, unified kingdom to a divided kingdom to no kingdom.

Imperceptible to those whose lives ebbed and flowed between these bookends of glory and disgrace (but not to us), the "mystery" of the Abrahamic promise and mission continued to unfold. Remember, this is *not* just ancient Near Eastern history. It is *our* history as well.

By the time Act III concludes and the lights dim, Zerubbabel had rebuilt the Temple under the prophetic warnings of Haggai and Zechariah, and Nehemiah was rebuilding the wall around Jerusalem while the prophet Malachi was trumpeting the need for covenant faithfulness. Ezra bolstered the people's hopes and identity through covenant renewal. Act III closes with a cryptic promise of a second Elijah joining the Story. And then, as in all compelling dramas, it's time for an Intermission.

13 Intermission: The Story's "Missing Page"

I have always marveled at how deftly and efficiently stage crews work their magic between acts. What was an elegant British mansion when the curtains close can be magically transformed into a quaint peasant cottage when they reopen. Stage transformations have been a challenge throughout history. It took seven hours for the Roman Colosseum to be transformed into an aquatic battleground by the "mere" addition of four million gallons of water from a redirected aqueduct. An amazing feat. But what Yahweh accomplished during His Intermission was so magnificent that roughly four centuries of silence seems too short for all that got put into place.[1]

For instance, the curtain on Act III *closes* with these words:

> Behold, I will send you Elijah the prophet before the great and awesome day of the LORD comes. And he will turn the hearts of fathers to their children and the hearts of children to their fathers, lest I come and strike the land with a decree of utter destruction. (Malachi 4:5–6)

And the curtain on Act IV *opens* with the introduction of John the Baptizer, right where Malachi left off in Act III during the days of Nehemiah, seemingly without skipping a beat:

> "[speaking of John] …and he will turn many of the children of Israel to the Lord their God, and he will go before him in the spirit and power of Elijah, to turn the hearts of the fathers to the children, and the

disobedient to the wisdom of the just, to make ready for the Lord a people prepared." (Luke 1:16–17)

At least a four-century Intermission separates these two comments. What happened backstage is vital to the continuation of the Story itself; it is crucial to understanding the rest of it—our New Testament.

In the closing scenes of Act III, we witnessed the rise and fall of the Hebrew monarchy, and we listened to sixteen prophets whose words make up nearly half of the Old Testament. In our preoccupation with the storyline of Scripture, we are tempted to assume that its storyline *is* the whole Story. It's not. Though its contents are sufficient, they are hardly exhaustive.[2] The Story we've been looking at—this "plan for the fullness of time," this "mystery hidden for ages"—is the *composite* of Yahweh's "ways." Even with the amazing help provided by the Bible, we must continually remind ourselves that the Story must be comprehensive enough to contain all people of all time. Its inscrutable nature has not changed simply because He has given us *some* of its details. Because the Story exists in the mind of Yahweh, it *exceeds* the boundaries of the Bible—though when we journey there, we have to do so without any help from Him. Put another way, the Story is immensely bigger than the Bible, so all history that is *not* in the Bible is still in the Story. And that means we're always missing something. The "gaps" in what can be known should keep us humble as we present this Story to others.

This means the nations with cameo appearances in the story of Israel are still important to Yahweh. The rise and fall of the Assyrians, Neo-Babylonians, and Persians all play enormous roles in Act III. However, their combined ink would occupy less than a single chapter in our Bible. A Persian king whom Yahweh calls His "anointed one" was responsible for keeping the Story alive by financing a return trip to the rubble of Jerusalem for 50,000 Jews.[3] They rejoiced at the thought of being allowed to return to their homeland, not knowing the role they were playing in the Story. We now know they were part of the "stage crew," rebuilding the city and its Temple, fulfilling their role so that Yahweh's plan for the fullness of time might continue.

Then, in Act IV, new key character groups are suddenly on stage in the four Gospels—Pharisees, Sadducees, and Herodians—and a single family (the Herods) dominates the lives of the people in the first five books of our New Testament. "Synagogues" and the sophisticated system of leadership and liturgy that comes with them appear everywhere. Yet none of this historical context is mentioned in our Old Testament! They were all carefully and strategically put into place by Yahweh during the Intermission. While the curtains on the Story were closed, Yahweh was directing three extraordinarily significant cultural highways that would converge about the time ACT IV begins. We'll call them the Greek, Roman, and Jewish.

The Greek Chapter

Our record of the Story fades in the books of Ezra and Nehemiah, with Artaxerxes as the ruler of the vast Persian Empire. But as we just said, the Bible *contains* the Story, but itself is not the *complete* Story. World history provides us with what transpired after our record went blank. In the fourth century BC, a usurper to the throne of Persia named Darius III found himself facing one of the most brilliant military commanders in history—Alexander the Great. The son of Philip II of Macedon, young Alexander was bent on owning the world. The result was the death of Darius III by his people and the end of Persia as a world power.

Alexander's empire was not long, but his meteoric rise would play an enormous role in setting the stage for Act IV. As a pupil of Aristotle, Alexander had a passion for learning. He carried copies of the *Iliad* and the *Odyssey* on military campaigns. He had an agenda of making Greek culture the new normal, and for the first time in history, the "West" was the dominant cultural force in the ancient Near East. Alexander built the world's most extensive library in Egypt, in a city he conveniently named for himself—Alexandria. Apollos, a brilliant disciple in our New Testament, was from Alexandria and undoubtedly studied in Alexander's library.[4] And Stephen, the first martyr for the gospel, was stoned after arguing with Greek-speaking Jews who were educated in Alexandria.[5] Even Paul felt the influence of Alexander. The two ships on which he sailed to Rome as a prisoner were likely built in the harbors of Alexandria.[6]

Alexander's two most lasting legacies are both unwitting contributions to Yahweh's Story. The first was his drive to unify the known world under the umbrella of Greek culture and learning. The second, which would be the vehicle of the first, was to spread the knowledge of the Greek language. He was highly successful in both. The Greek language became the *lingua franca* of the known world, especially in the Mediterranean Basin, which became the radiating center for the Story's movement to the *goyim* (the nations). The Jewish scriptures were translated from Hebrew to Greek in Alexandria. Some aristocratic Jews of

Jesus' day (the Sadducees) embraced Greek culture and much of its philosophy.

Yahweh didn't desire that the whole world *become* Greek. That was Alexander's passion. But it's safe to say that Yahweh did want the entire world to *know* Greek. Alexander's ambition was a vital part of the Story. By the time of Paul's conversion, 350 years later, a universal language was already in place, enabling Paul and others to spread the news of Jesus and the "mystery of the kingdom" everywhere.

Alexander's ambition to unite the known world also promoted the ground-breaking notion that a single family could be composed of various ethnicities. This is at the heart of the mystery hidden for ages. Alexander, again unwittingly, laid the foundation for the radical words that Paul would utter centuries later:

> But now in Christ Jesus you who once were far off have been brought near by the blood of Christ. For he himself is our peace, who has made us both one and has broken down in his flesh the dividing wall of hostility by abolishing the law of commandments expressed in ordinances, that *he might create in himself one new man in place of the two*, so making peace, and might reconcile us both to God in one body through the cross, thereby killing the hostility. (Ephesians 2:12–16)

The universal church, or the Body of Christ, emerged in a tribally-oriented world that had been prepared by a brilliant pagan in the fourth century before Jesus. In a very ironic way, what Christians affirm in the Apostles' Creed— "I believe in the holy catholic [universal] church: the communion of saints"—owes *something* of its acceptance in the first century to Alexander's vision of a more homogenous culture.

In short, the Greek contribution during our Intermission is enormous. From it, we are bequeathed our New Testament. It also helped push us in the direction of the relational unity that characterized life before the Fall of Man.

The Roman Chapter

The second cultural influence that prepared the way for Act IV was Rome. This Republic-turned-Empire vanquished the crippled kingdom that Alexander left behind after his death. In 63 BC, the Roman commander Pompey conquered Jerusalem and squashed the corrupt Jewish priest-king dynasty that had emerged from the ashes of Alexander's empire scattered there by one of his generals,

Seleucus, three centuries earlier. A non-Jew named Antipater switched sides during the tumultuous era of Rome's move from republic to empire. In the process, he also endeared himself to the Hasmoneans, the Jewish priestly family ruling in Jerusalem at the time. When Rome finally squashed what remained of a Jewish "kingdom," Antipater found himself the benefactor of both of his associations.

This is all very important because one of Antipater's sons, and *his* descendants, cast a long shadow over the biblical landscape for the next three generations. We know him as Herod the Great.

This is the Herod who is credited with the infamous "massacre of the innocents"—the wholesale killing of children two years and younger—in his frantic attempt to destroy the one called "the King of the Jews." This same Herod is responsible for the beautifully renovated Temple in which Jesus would eventually teach and cause trouble. This same Herod built a spell-binding artificial port on the Mediterranean coast named Caesarea, to which Peter would bring the gospel to a Gentile named Cornelius and from which Paul would sail under guard for Rome. Herod was still dealing from both sides of the deck, trying to placate the Jews and Rome with his world-class construction projects.

Herod's personal life was worthy of daytime television. His privileged children were educated in Rome, and Herod himself was close to Augustus, Rome's first emperor. This baby-killer was in the elite class, comfortable with the movers and shakers of his day. However, he was only a puppet on Rome's larger stage and, as a non-Jew, a suspicious outsider at best to the true descendants of Abraham living in Jerusalem.

Rome's real presence in Palestine was in the form of a series of prefects, or governors, who were appointed to rule an unruly people. The fifth prefect is history's best known. His name was Pontius Pilate, a man memorialized in the Apostles' Creed I quoted above.

In the time of Yeshua, everything bore the Roman imprint. Tax collectors, currency, legions, officers, and judgment halls dotted the land like date palms. One could not travel five miles in any direction without a temptation to think that Rome, not Yahweh, ruled the world, especially this little corner of it. If the vision under Alexander was a Greek world, the vision of Rome was domination through war. So instead of providing universal language, Rome's legacy to the first century had to do with military expansion and aristocratic prominence—and roadways. Militaristic regimes need troops to move to protect their borders. They also need to stimulate commerce and collect taxes to bankroll their ideology. Rome did this by building paved roads, some 50,000 miles of them throughout the empire. Little did the rulers in Rome realize they were constructing Yahweh's highways for the gospel to travel down centuries later. Paul and the rest of the missionary movement emanating from Jerusalem relied heavily upon the Roman road system in their efforts to bring the *musterion* (the "mystery") to the nations.

Roman law also allowed Paul to move with near impunity through the legal bureaucracies of the Roman cities in which he often found himself in danger. More than once, he used his citizenship as a "get out of jail free" card.[7]

But perhaps the most significant way Yahweh employed His Roman stage crew during the Intermission was in the *pax Romana*, 180 years of relative peace. With the end of the wars surrounding the fall of the Republic, Augustus initiated this time of relative calm. Today, it's impossible to imagine Jesus being born in Bethlehem! Now a Palestinian territory, Joseph and Mary would not even be allowed access to the city!

Rome's contribution to the stage was safe and efficient travel, a just system of laws, and a season of relative international peace. There is one more cultural influence to note during this Story's interlude…

The Jewish Chapter

A final contributor during the Intermission was made by Yahweh's own chosen people, the Jews. When we read the New Testament, we sometimes rush to get through the Gospels. Our journey hastens to Paul—his letters and his ministry to the Gentiles. In the rush, we totally forget that the early church was *Jewish*—thoroughly Jewish. The original center of the faith was not Rome or Antioch, but Jerusalem. The first converts were all Jews, as were the apostles themselves. The converts on Pentecost—three thousand of them—were all Jews. When Paul entered a city on a missionary journey, his first target audience was always Jews.

Yahweh used the Jews in the Story by strategically redistributing them before the curtain closed on Act III. The relocation policies of the Assyrians in their destruction of the northern ten tribes of Israel in the eighth century BC, and the deportation tactics of the Babylonians in their annihilation of the Temple and the two southern tribes 200 years later both served Yahweh's purposes. When it came time for the curtain to reopen for Act IV, Jews were scattered throughout the known world. Thanks to Luke's Book of Acts, we have eye-witness accounts of this reality at Pentecost, some six hundred years *after* the dispersions:

> And at this sound the multitude came together, and they were bewildered, because each one was hearing them speak in his own language. And they were amazed and astonished, saying, "Are not all these who are speaking Galileans? And how is it that we hear, each of us in his own native language? Parthians and Medes and Elamites and residents of Mesopotamia, Judea and Cappadocia, Pontus and Asia, Phrygia and Pamphylia, Egypt and the parts of Libya belonging to Cyrene, and visitors from Rome, both Jews and proselytes, Cretans and Arabians—we hear them telling in our own tongues the mighty works of God." (Acts 2:6–11)

Another Jewish contribution during the Intermission centered on how they worshiped after they left Egypt. Yahweh had informed Moses in Act III that His people would be limited to a single shrine in a single city. This was a necessary deterrent to the rampant idolatry and multi-god worship that characterized the surrounding nations. However, the pull of culture has always been the silent enemy of Yahweh's purposes, and His people became idolators. As He had warned repeatedly through the prophets, the Temple was finally destroyed at the hands of the Babylonians in the early 6th century BC. This devastating event cut the soul out of a people whose identity was inseparable from their ritual. Because they were detached from their Temple and the sacrificial system it provided, multiple local venues of worship had to be created. These sacred places—synagogues—helped assuage this loss, but they were no replacement for the single national shrine of Yahweh that had been their place of worship in Jerusalem. For ardent Jews, synagogues were a poor substitute for the Temple, but they did provide a unique sense of identity in the cities where they dwelt as "strangers and exiles."

Only in retrospect can we see God's larger purposes in the demolition of the first Temple. In its destruction, Yahweh didn't merely judge His people for their idolatry as He promised in His covenant with them. This second "diaspora" of Jews created a network of starting points for Paul and others like him to spread the message of the mystery of the Kingdom from Jerusalem to Judea and Samaria…and the ends of the earth.

The list goes on. Another way Yahweh was able to draw His elect people into the Story was their expectation of a Messiah. The Jews didn't need to be educated about Jesus' appearance. Unlike the Greeks and Romans, they were already *expecting* a Messiah. It was part of Jewish theology and life. Their problem would be with the mission of Yeshua and his claims about himself. This explained why the early apostles were tasked with proving to the Jews how a *crucified* Messiah truly did fit their prophetic model.

Another evidence of Jewish preparation for the gospel during the Intermission is obvious in Paul's ministry. His discussions with Greeks (like the philosophers in Acts 17) stand in stark contrast to his arguments with Orthodox Jews everywhere he went. The Jews had a place in their thinking for a Messiah, the resurrection, and a God who was in the habit of revealing Himself personally. In addition to their elaborate mythology, the Romans had deified the emperor, while the Greeks had a pantheon of gods and goddesses. In short, the "learning curve" for Jews in Act IV and V would be small. But so would be their tolerance for the scandalous message that the long-awaited Messiah not only *died*, but He did so for Gentiles as much as for Jews!

Okay, so the lights are flickering and it's time to return to our seats. Hopefully after the Intermission you feel a little better informed. Unless you are a history buff, it's not likely that you will remember everything we marched through, but your takeaway is that Act IV of the Story was drastically shaped "offstage" by three disparate cultures: Greek, Roman, and Jewish. When the curtains reopen for Act IV, we will discover we are at a climax, for "...the fullness of time had come, God sent forth his Son, born of woman, born under the law."[8]

And as the Story resumes, something is stirring behind the curtain. It's through an eccentric desert preacher, fulfilling the words of an ancient prophecy: "Prepare the way of the Lord, make his paths straight."[9] It is impossible for us living in the twenty-first century to fathom the tumultuous effect of this voice breaking the silence of ten generations! This was as significant as the thunder the Jews heard when Moses was on top of Mount Sinai. At long last, Yahweh was speaking to His people again.

14 Act IV — Climax

John the Apostle tells us that the "world itself could not contain the books" if one were to record all that Jesus taught and did.¹ Accepting that wise counsel, I surely won't attempt to prove him wrong in this brief chapter!

In our five-act Story, Act IV is by far the most important. It is the highpoint and the fulcrum of all history. Everything either leads up to Act IV or flows from it. Nothing in the Story has any purpose apart from it. As we learned earlier, Yahweh has "a plan (plot) for the fullness of time (*kairos*), to unite all things in him [Jesus], things in heaven and things on earth." In Act IV, the "Him" of that plan steps onto the stage that Yahweh had been building for four centuries!

If you are thinking of a domesticated nativity scene, please throw that image away. The drive-thru versions in which the sheep and donkey have more curb appeal than the Savior just doesn't match the facts. This Story is real. It's filled with irony. And what greater irony could there be than the fact that while the Herods and Caesars were living in opulence, the God of the universe made His incarnate entrance in an obscure barn in Bethlehem.

Luke's purpose for including a detailed birth narrative in his Gospel must have had something to do with its significance in the Story. I don't think he's trying to give us a family album of Jesus' childhood. Everyone who encountered this Child found themselves, in one fashion or another, on their knees before Him.² From a woman's womb, the God of *kairos* stepped into *chronos*. In the words of John the Apostle, Yahweh had "pitched His tent" amid the sons and daughters of Adam. A new type of "Temple" appeared. Jerusalem's Temple was merely a prototype.³ In an event as universe-tilting as the sin of our First Parents, deity took on flesh. If there is a list of Yahweh's "ways" that are not *our* "ways," surely this event is near the top. The Creator had become a creature. The Potter became a pot. It turns out, the manger at the opening of Act IV was far more humiliating for Jesus than the cross at the end of it. But I'm getting ahead of myself.

After the long downward spiral that started in Act II, hope is finally introduced into the Story. But before we can fully understand what happens in Act IV, we've got to add yet another Story word to the grammar we created at the beginning. And that is "good news" or "gospel" as it is called in our New Testament.

We've talked about this good news as it relates to our sanctification. We've also talked about it in relationship to Paul's conversation. But let's take it a little further. The English word *gospel* in our Bible is cut from a very different cloth than other familiar words, such as *baptize* or *king*. And I think this sets us off in the wrong direction from the start. For example, *baptize* is merely the English transliteration of the Greek verb *baptizō*, and *king* has a one-to-one correlation with the same idea in the Greek language. But the English word *gospel* in our Bibles has its roots in Olde English, *not* Greek. It is derived from *gōdspel* ("good" + "story"), which over time was reduced to *gospel*.

Unfortunately, for most modern Christians, their understanding of *gospel* is vacant of any idea of "story," much less the One Story. Instead, *gospel* has become a synonym for an abbreviated evangelistic method. We then superimpose our meaning for *gospel* backwards onto every occurrence of it in scripture. So, when we read that Paul was "not ashamed of the gospel" (Romans 1:16), we might envision him sharing some first-century version of an evangelistic pamphlet. But that cheapens the Story. It's too big, too old, and too rich to be reduced to a PowerPoint slide and a prayer.

In our New Testament, the word *euaggelion* (the Greek word translated as "gospel") has two sides. One side is a verb—the activity of "proclaiming" or "preaching." The flipside is a noun—the *content* of that preaching. And we are repeatedly told this content is "good news" of some kind. In contrast to the modern four-points-and-a-prayer approach, the "gospel" in the four Gospels has less to do with the forgiveness of sins and more to do with the *announcement* of a major plot-line shift within the Story.

John the Baptizer and Yeshua made unbreakable connections between the "good news" (i.e., the gospel) and something they both called the "kingdom of God" that had broken into time and space. And whatever this "kingdom" was, it's obviously something people have been longing for, and thus its arrival is hailed as good news, a "good story," or *gōdspel*, if you will. And we know that it is not just a "good" story; it is a mystery hidden for ages, a "plan for the fullness of time." It's the One Story of the One God.

Mark, in his signature abbreviated style, distills it best, attributing the "good news" to Yahweh, and linking the Kingdom, the "fullness of time," with the gospel: "Now after John was arrested, Jesus came into Galilee, proclaiming the gospel of God, and saying, 'The time is fulfilled, and the kingdom of God is at hand; repent and believe in the gospel.'"[4]

Don't miss me here. The message of forgiveness of sins *is* a dominant theme throughout the Gospels, running from start to finish.[5] But the forgiveness of sins is never associated with the word *gospel* in the Gospels. In fact, there isn't a single place in the New Testament where *gospel* and *sin*, or *gospel* and *forgiveness*, appear in the same verse! The "good news" in the Gospels is directed more to the poor, the sick, and "the nations" than it is the guilty.[6]

When we equate the "gospel" with news about justification from sin and guilt, our gaze slowly turns from the Story to ourselves. "Faith" is understood as the pathway to justification (*my* justification), instead of a life of submission to the One Story. As we said way back in the beginning, this two-dimensional understanding hoards our faith for ourselves and those like us.

Paul understood this. He opened and closed Romans (his most thorough and theological letter) on the topic of the "gospel." Here we see that "faith" is infinitely more significant than mere personal belief:

> [opening] Paul, a servant of Christ Jesus, called to be an apostle, set apart for the gospel of God, which he promised beforehand through his prophets in the holy Scriptures, concerning his Son, who was descended from David according to the flesh and was declared to be the Son of God in power according to the Spirit of holiness by his resurrection from the dead, Jesus Christ our Lord, through whom *we have received grace and apostleship to bring about* **the obedience of faith** *for the sake of his name among all the nations,* including you who are called to belong to Jesus Christ...

> [closing] Now to him who is able to strengthen you according to my

> gospel and the preaching of Jesus Christ, according to the revelation of the mystery that was kept secret for long ages but has now been disclosed and through the prophetic writings *has been made known to all nations, according to the command of the eternal God, to bring about* **the obedience of faith**—to the only wise God be glory forevermore through Jesus Christ! Amen. (Romans 1:1–6; 16:25–27)

To make faith private and personal, instead of public and behavioral, is to heist ACT IV from the rest of the Story and plug it into a story of our own. Whenever faith becomes privatized, the Story will inevitably be hijacked by whatever narrative is popular within the church at the time. Why? Because somewhere along the line we were told that the gospel is, "God loves *you* and has a wonderful plan (story) for *your* life." The forgiveness of sins is surely one of the *benefits* of the "good news." But it isn't the good news itself. The gospel is the proclamation of a kingdom arriving, not just sins departing.

The four Gospels (ACT IV) in their larger Story context introduce an event in a Story that's *older* than Jesus and more expansive than the Jews. The Gospels explain the fuller meaning of Acts I–III and create the context for Act V. And they do so in a way that is consistent with the Abrahamic blessing and mission. Is it any wonder that Matthew opens his Gospel by reaching back from Jesus to Abraham and closes it with Yeshua sending his disciples to "the nations?"[7] It turns out, what we call the Great Commission—taking the "good news" to the nations—began with Yahweh talking to Abraham in Canaan, not Jesus talking to His disciples in Galilee.

> Those of faith are the sons of Abraham! And the Scripture, foreseeing that God would justify the Gentiles by faith, preached the gospel beforehand to Abraham, saying, "In you shall all the nations be blessed." So then, those who are of faith are blessed along with Abraham, the man of faith. (Galatians 3:7–9)

Perhaps this is why Matthew's narrative interpreted Jesus' life and ministry as the *fulfillment of prophecy* at least fifteen times. For Matthew, the "trailers" of the Old Testament were being fulfilled in Jesus. Our only Gentile author, Luke, also put Abraham on center stage, mentioning him twice as often as Matthew who was a Jew. Even Paul, whom many perceive as lobbying against the Mosaic Law, apparently believed Abraham to be a more central figure to the "gospel" than

Moses. He referred to him twice as often in his letters.[8] Jesus' cryptic statement to the Jewish elders, "Your father Abraham *rejoiced* that he would see my day. He saw it and was glad,"[9] makes sense because of the shared purpose between himself and Abraham.

In Act IV, the time had come. *Kairos* had become intertwined with *chronos*. The mystery hidden for ages would be disclosed. *Everything* had been leading up to this event. Jesus knew and accepted this. He clarified His own leading role in the Story and exposed our tendency to miss the larger picture.

> And he said to them, "O foolish ones, and slow of heart to believe all that the prophets have spoken! Was it not necessary that the Christ should suffer these things and enter into his glory?" *And beginning with Moses and all the Prophets, he interpreted to them in all the Scriptures the things concerning himself.* . . .

But perhaps the clearest statement from Yeshua to his contemporaries about missing the point—one that has special application for us and this book—is in His rebuke to the religious elite of His day:

> "And the Pharisees and Sadducees came, and to test him they asked him to show them a sign from heaven. He answered them, "When it is evening, you say, 'It will be fair weather, for the sky is red.' And in the morning, 'It will be stormy today, for the sky is red and threatening.' *You know how to interpret the appearance of the sky, but you cannot interpret the signs of the times* [kairos]." (Matthew 16:1–3)

Seeing the Gospels as Act IV of an unbroken Story, instead of the first four books of a "New Testament," is so important. I fear that many of us are like the Levite in the parable of the Good Samaritan who ran past the injured man in a hurry to Jerusalem. We rush past Good Friday to get to Easter, and I suspect we sprint through the Gospels to get to Golgotha and the empty tomb. Unfortunately, in the process, we run right past the eternal purposes of God. This is because we're thinking in terms of *our story*. But this isn't unique to us. The Jews of Yeshua's day did the same thing.

So, as we look at Act IV, we must retire the notion that the four Gospels exist to tell us the "good news" that our sins are forgiven so that we can have a personal savior and private salvation. Jesus lived 33 years—not 33 hours. Why?

What was the point of His life before His crucifixion?

Thy Kingdom Come, Thy Will Be Done

When Jesus first appeared as the Messiah in His home synagogue, He read a passage that wove together the Messiah, the good news, and the poor and oppressed.[10] These were all common Jewish themes, but they were typically associated with the end of all things. They were the hope of first-century Jews, yet they were part of a distant future for most. But on that Sabbath day in the synagogue, as Jesus rolled up the Isaiah scroll and handed it back to the attendant, He asserted, "Today this Scripture has been fulfilled in your hearing."[11]

The fallout from that statement is an indicator of just how deeply ingrained these messianic longings were. Some in attendance were ecstatic, suddenly realizing that the hope of the ages might be birthed in their lifetime. Maybe in their very midst! But others were downright hostile. They had missed the first press release of the mystery because it wasn't what they expected. Yahweh wasn't who they thought He was. And apparently neither was Jesus. One author connects this reality with another unavoidable truth in the Gospels: Jesus' target audience was *not* the rich and illustrious but the needy and uneducated.

> Jesus, telling stories about a sower sowing seeds, about weeds among the wheat, and about a vineyard where the tenants refuse to give the owner the fruit, is allowing these ancient echoes to take root in the fertile and scripture-soaked minds of his hearers, to try to get through to them the message that what they have longed for is happening at last, but it doesn't look as they thought it would! God is at last doing the great new thing he's always promised for Israel—but the wrong people seem to be getting the message, and many of the right people are missing it entirely![12]

This case of mistaken identity runs throughout the four Gospels. Eventually, it will lead some angry Jews to Pilate to seek Jesus' murder and draw others to Jesus to seek his Kingdom. Because the Story wasn't "their" story, many missed God in skin when He came to town. But those who had *no* story—the poor and powerless—were spellbound as He unveiled what the arrival of this Kingdom would look like. With every parable that began with, "The Kingdom of God is like…" their plot hunger was slaked. For them, this definitely *was* "good news."

As we work our way through the Gospel narratives, we see perplexity growing alongside hostility. Even Yeshua's entrance into Jerusalem on Palm Sunday was a mixed metaphor. He was hailed as a king yet rode on a donkey's colt, a symbol of peace, not victory.[13] Matthew, reflecting years later, informs his readers that this event was a fulfillment of a fifth-century BC "trailer."[14]

A common laborer riding a baby donkey was not what the Jews anticipated for the one to shatter Rome's yoke. But how could they know that Jesus' mission was *not* to save the Jews from Rome? They had long forgotten that the Abrahamic mission extended beyond the gene pool of Israel. Jesus had come to bring a Kingdom that was "not of this world." But even this is hidden from their sight; it will take Saul-become-Paul in Act V to guide believers to see the unbroken connection between Adam in Eden, Abraham in Ur, and Jesus in Jerusalem. This was new wine indeed. But not everyone had the new skins to contain it.

The atonement for sin that occurred on Calvary's cross enabled humanity and God to be reconciled at last, just as Jesus had promised.[15] But it also marked a turning point in a conflict that began in Eden. Rome was not the enemy, merely a pawn of the real Enemy. What happened that ancient Friday, when the souls of the Jewish hopeful were ripped in half along with the Temple curtain, was *not* just that humanity's debt was paid. It was, and that is surely good news! *But it isn't the gospel.* The *real* "good news" always has to do with the *Kingdom*, not its subjects.

In speaking of His impending crucifixion, Jesus said, "Now is the judgment of this world; now will the ruler of this world be cast out."[16] That meant the oldest "trailer" on record for Act IV, found near the end of Act II, was about to play itself out:

> The LORD God said to the serpent, "Because you have done this, cursed are you above all livestock and above all beasts of the field; on your belly you shall go, and dust you shall eat all the days of your life. I will put enmity between you and the woman, and between your offspring and her offspring; he shall bruise [crush] your head, and you shall bruise his heel." (Genesis 3:14–15)

Those who boasted that they knew Yahweh and His purposes were in for a surprise. Even those who were truly "looking for the kingdom," including John the Baptizer himself, seemed to grow more and more confused by Jesus' obvious intention *not* to restore the throne of David.[17] As Act IV unfolded, the hostile minority trumped the confused majority. By the time Good Friday arrived, less than a week after Palm Sunday's "triumphal entry," Jesus was abandoned on a Roman cross, His accusers present and His disciples absent, except for John and a few women. And from this final pulpit, Jesus cried out, "It is finished,"[18] the public proclamation of what He had said privately to His Father in prayer with His disciples the night before: "I have finished the work you gave me to do."[19]

This might sound anticlimactic. Here the Story just seems to stall out. The expectations of all Israel were hanging dead on a tree atop a desolate hill. We can only imagine the desecration of hope that spread through Jerusalem like a plague for those next two days. Jesus' last words, "It is finished," repeated countless times, as eyewitnesses rehearsed the events of that afternoon to those who were absent. All hope was past tense. Jesus was right. It really *was* "finished."

The Day Death Died

The one thing that had prevented the arrival of the Kingdom was Death. The threat looming over the Tree in Eden had ruled supreme and unchallenged since that infamous choice. And Death had been the victor on Calvary. How could there be a Kingdom? The King had died.

It *was* "finished," but it was not over. The Story doesn't end here.

No one could have imagined that Death itself could die. But die it did, early on the first day of that week. The death of Death has another name: *resurrection*. And resurrection marked the beginning of what was next in the Story—the coming of the Kingdom in power.

After ascending into heaven, Jesus "sat down at the right hand of God."[20] His reign as King began after His ascension. He is the King of Kings and Lord of Lords *now*, not eventually. No more mangers, no more swaddling clothes, no more nativity scenes. And from the throne of God, we hear a word from His lips that informs us that what happened on Calvary was bigger than sin and humanity: "And he who was seated on the throne said, 'Behold, I am making all things new.' Also, he said, 'Write this down, for these words are trustworthy and true.'"[21]

The work Jesus had "finished" made possible the work that was still to be done, the blessing of the nations. Jesus told His disciples that because He was returning to the Father, *they* would be able to continue "works" He had begun: "Truly, truly, I say to you, whoever believes in me will also do the works that I do; and greater works than these will he do, because I am going to the Father."[22]

Again, if we are looking at the whole picture of the Story, Yeshua's life is as important as his death. He says so Himself: "For even the Son of Man came not to be served but to serve, *and* to give his life as a ransom for many."[23] If we're not careful, we'll be preoccupied with his suffering, dying, and rising. We will miss the inseparable connection He repeatedly made between His *mission* as Messiah, and His *ministry* of feeding, touching, and healing![24]

Remember, we learned earlier that ministry is on the flipside of sanctification. It is where our own sanctification fits in the Story. Paul puts it very clear in Act V (which we'll get to shortly) when he says that we have been "…predestined to be conformed to the image of his Son, in order that he might be the firstborn among many brothers."[25] God's sanctification *of* us is not *for* us. He is raising up a veritable army of sons and daughters who resemble His Son. Why? So that we can "do the greater works" than Jesus did while we're here.[26] Beloved, genuine ministry is one of the few things we can do in this life that we can't in the next. There is no need for ministry on the new earth because there is no suffering. And there's no suffering because there's no sin. Ministry, the kind Jesus did, is for you and me, here and now.

The final moments of Act IV marked the beginning of something bigger than my forgiveness. It's true that the gospel *involves* me and my guilt, and justification is surely one of its blessings. But justification is not the gospel. The gospel is the announcement of the Kingdom: Calvary, the empty tomb, and the ascension of Yeshua to the throne of Yahweh. But it's not *about* me. It's about the Kingdom coming on earth as it is in heaven! And *that* is a "good Story," one that would surely be a blessing to all who hear it. It's a Story worth taking to the nations, which is exactly what happens in Act V.

15 ACT V — Culmination

Scene 1 (Acts through Jude)

Act V is the last act in the Story, and since it is the consummation of everything, it should be no surprise that it's long. So we're considering it in three scenes.

Scene 1 occupies the first 60 years of Act V, and it takes up a lot of ink (even more than Act III, which spanned 1,500 years from Abraham to Artaxerxes). Just as Act III makes up the bulk of the Old Testament, Act V occupies the majority of the New Testament. But the volume of ink is not a barometer of value. The life and ministry of Jesus of Act IV is still the centerpiece of the Story. And Jesus, not Paul, is the One Story's key figure. I am amazed and saddened by the relative unimportance placed on the words of Jesus compared to those of Paul. The purpose of Jesus was not to give Paul something to write about! As Jesus told Andrew, "Anyone who has seen me has seen the Father."[1] The writer of Hebrews tells us that "He is the radiance of the glory of God and the exact imprint of his nature."[2] Act IV (the four Gospels) gives us the clearest, most exhaustive, and final portrait we have of Yahweh in a body. Don't ever forget that. When reading the Bible during your lifetime, make sure that Act IV stays at the top of your list.

Luke, the largest contributor to the New Testament, helps bridge Act IV and Act V by putting the ascension of Jesus (and the events surrounding it) at the center of his two-volume effort, Luke and Acts. The ascension appears at the place both books nearly touch, the *end* of his Gospel and the *beginning* of his Book of Acts. This nearly seamless transition gives a beautiful continuity to the Story. We get Jesus' missional mandate to the apostles to go to the nations followed by his ascent to rule at the Father's right hand in both books. In Luke, it is Jesus' final command; in Acts, it is the introduction and outline to the book. The "Great Commission" as we call it, in Luke, is *not* a call to evangelize. It is a command to take the Story to the nations. In fact, this is the entire *purpose* of the Church, because it is the purpose of God. Not understanding this creates a two-dimensional understanding of Church, where getting people to "come to church" is seen as faithfulness to the Great Commission. God doesn't have a mission for His Church, so much as He has created a Church for His mission. Mission was not made for the Church; the Church was made for mission—God's mission.[3]

Understanding the equivalence between the Abrahamic Mission and the mission of the Church is the only way we can stop putting *ourselves* into the gospel. It also curtails any community of believers trying to "brand" their unique church. The refusal to see it this way is at the heart of tribalism among Christians. A "market share" approach to ministry prevents churches and individuals from locking arms and pooling resources to bring the Story to the nations. God has never negotiated with His people regarding what *they* felt their mission should be. He never will. There is only one mission because there is only one Story. The more we and the people in the pews with us on Sundays understand this, the more we are truly the Church—the "family of God." The "many brothers" of which Jesus is the firstborn.

And of course, the inverse is also true. Scholar and author Christopher Wright takes it a step further and *disqualifies* any group from being the Church if it refuses to submit to the One Story: "In this age, the church is missional or it is not the church."[4]

In Scene 1 of Act V, we see the first example of a perennial struggle for God's new family. God asks a predominantly Jewish church to accept that Judaism and the Law of Moses were temporary, and to embrace the eternal purpose of Yahweh to fulfill the blessing of Abraham to *all* people groups. Luke's Book of Acts provides the chronological matrix within which most of Paul's letters were written. Between Luke and Paul, we can construct a picture of the spread of the good news from Jewish Jerusalem, to biracial Samaria, and on to "the nations," (the Gentiles living around the Mediterranean Basin). As we've said, Luke's account gives us the transformation of Paul in full color. It also includes the martyrdoms of Stephen and James and the early persecution of believers.

But there's one more significant thing. Here we see a role reversal in the narrative — the withdrawal of Jesus and the preeminence of the Holy Spirit. The Holy Spirit will be big in this book, averaging two appearances per chapter, more than any other book in the New Testament. So we are front-row spectators as the good news moves in concentric circles from the place where Jesus was last seen to parts of the world He had never visited. We learn of radical conversions, churches planted, and ultimately a new "chosen people," a new family drawn from the social strata the Jews were careful to exclude:

> For as many of you as were baptized into Christ have put on Christ. There is neither Jew nor Greek, there is neither slave nor free, there is no male and female, for you are all one in Christ Jesus. And if you are Christ's, then you are Abraham's offspring, heirs according to promise. (Galatians 3:27–29)

> [You] have put on the new self, which is being renewed in knowledge after the image of its creator. Here there is not Greek and Jew, circumcised and uncircumcised, barbarian, Scythian, slave, free; but Christ is all, and in all. (Colossians 3:10–11)

Some people have called Act V, Scene 1 the "Apostolic Age" because the movement was led by men and women connected to the original disciples trained by Jesus. Luke gives us a partial record of their movements in Acts, and the remainder of Scene 1 provides us with much of their correspondence to various churches. These remaining letters, which themselves claim divine inspiration, constitute the majority of our New Testament.[5] Our doctrine of the inspiration of Scripture demands that we ascribe to them the same status we give to the Old Testament.

However, we should note that some improv was happening in at this point.[6] The Jewish Law had worship and obedience down to a science, but this "gospel to the nations" was virgin territory. The coming of the Holy Spirit in power at Pentecost meant things got messier…and it stayed that way throughout the narrative in the Book of Acts.

For most first-century Jews, the only good Samaritan was a dead one. But Jewish believers now had to fellowship with biracial Samaritans who also claimed to be in the family. Jesus never gave specifics on this one! The Story seems to burst all conventional boundaries much like Jesus' parable about putting new wine into old wine skins. We read of these believers embracing anyone who would respond, regardless of gender, social standing, ethnicity, or sexual orientation.[7] You can almost hear them saying to each another, "Where is this all going?" You can almost feel the heat of those early debates.

Fortunately, Scene 1 of Act V is directed by Spirit-led, apostolic leadership. It was new territory for everyone, but they had some veteran apostles to help as they worked their way into the unknown. We have inherited the byproduct of their efforts—our New Testament.

So that brings us to the next scene of Act V. What's left is very, very important. Remember, God's word to us was first God's word to someone else. We must continually remind ourselves of this as we read the inspired letters in the Bible. They were written by Spirit-led apostles, speaking into specific contemporary circumstances, seeking to assist the newcomers to this Story idea. Just as we agreed about prophetic passages, we must read our New Testament *in context*. These letters are brilliantly insightful and contain timeless truths that spill beyond the boundaries of their time. But they aren't a "handbook" for church planting. Instead, our New Testament is an amazing *record* of Spirit-led improvisation when it came to fulfilling the mandate Jesus gave as he left. Knowing that, how could we not be humble as we try to apply this to our lives in the twenty-first century? Our certainty without humility is rightly interpreted by the watching world as arrogance. As we will see in the next scene, this improv necessity should keep us on our knees.

Scene 2 (The Here and Now)

Scene 2 of Act V is basically a continuation of Scene 1, with one significant difference—no one who had walked with and known Jesus is still alive. A major setback. Unless you're Yahweh.

Those living in Scene 1 could at least draw from the letters that were circulating or talk to the apostles that were still living. But this isn't true for Scene 2. When it comes to the Bible's record of the Story, this is the *only* part of it where the Scriptures are silent. The New Testament is a record of Scene 1, but Scene 2 is where we find ourselves right now! And there's no script. No flesh and blood eyewitnesses to lead the way.

Whenever I teach on this topic, I can feel the collective anxiety of realizing that we are "flying blind" in a sense. My point here is huge, but its importance has more to do with how we *do* ministry, not how good we are *at* it. And, if you've been around folks in ministry as much as I have over the years, you know that many of us *act* as though we really know what God is doing. But the inconvenient truth (something anyone who's been engaged in significant ministry for any length of time knows) is this: *we haven't got a clue what we're doing!*

God doesn't have a Twitter feed or a Facebook page. He's not in the business of live updates on how the Story is going. And buried deep within His sovereignty is the freedom He has granted people to make choices, which He seems to honor. There is at least *some* evidence in history that Christians make mistakes, can't get along, and take their Adamic residue to church. As I said, we have no clue what we're doing for the Story, in the Story, or to the Story!

This is compounded by an Enlightenment gene that wormed its way into American Christianity sometime after the eighteenth century. More than any other religious tradition, we seem to be obsessed with a need to *tell* people what God is "doing" in our lives. We also expect others to give us a report on their own Christian experience. I'll never forget someone asking me what God was "teaching" me through two family divorces, my mother's death, and a personal bout with cancer complete with complications. I felt a wave of embarrassment crawl across my soul when something didn't immediately come to mind. I guess I assumed that for an inquiry as "spiritual" as this, *something* should immediately present itself, sort of like an appointment on my smartphone. But nothing did. Staring blankly at the person, I confessed, "I don't know."

He looked at me as though God must have sent a memo, and I missed it. Something deep inside me wanted to respond a little more aggressively, like, "How could I *possibly* know the answer to that?"

Now, before you judge me, let me update that report. Of course, cancer brought me back to square one. Of course, cancer fueled my prayer life. Of course, cancer gave me more compassion for others who've suffered the same. Of course cancer rocked my world and drove me to God. And the combination of that with the divorces, death, and about five other things I failed to mention turned my heart inside out. But to be asked to report on what *God* was "teaching me," I really couldn't say. *He* hadn't told me.

Surely I could come up with *something* to report. And that's what we do, don't we? We find something. At least that's what I did that day. I lied. I'm a Bible teacher for crying out loud. I'm *supposed* to have an answer to a question like that. But the bottom line is—I didn't know. And I still don't. I *do* know I'm not the same person. I *do* know that God's deafening silence at a time of great need caused me to struggle in a new way with His goodness *and* His God-ness. I *do* know that the pain wore away my thin little Jesus veneer and besieged my previous quick-to-respond reporting of what God was "doing" or "saying" in my life. But to attribute something to *God* with certainty? There was no burning bush, just the warm feeling of brokenness while having a quiet time or weeping. And if I *don't* have an answer, is it pride or fear that prompts me to respond as if I do? Wouldn't it be richer and more honoring to Him to simply say, "I'm not sure. But here are some things I now know…" or something similar that's a bit more honest and truer to reality?

This does *not* mean we should be hopeless or conclude that we are helpless. Or that God doesn't make some things very clear. However, it does mean that we should be humble, both in life and in ministry. It means that we take ownership of the Adamic residue that wants to be first, wants to be right, wants to be noticed. It demands that we *listen* to others when they speak into our lives. Our submission *to* the Story always has priority over any contribution we want to make *in* it.

To do otherwise, to pretend always to know, is pride all dressed up and ready for church. This is serious because God said that He opposes the proud.[8] He is *against* them, not merely disappointed with them. And to make matters worse, when it comes to spiritual progress or ministry, pride dams up grace. It prevents it from flowing. If there's anything we Christians need, it's grace. And if there's anything we don't need, it's pride. Admitting that we don't always know what God is "doing," "teaching," or "asking" might be a step in the direction of spiritual maturity.

So, Scene 2 is where we live. It's the "in-between" time since the death of the Apostle John on the Island of Patmos, and the return of the King riding on a white horse in the Book of Revelation. We live in the "here, but not yet" portion of the Story. And it's a tough place to pitch your tent, because like the early church, we are improvising, but *unlike* the early church, the apostles have all left the building. Paul, a latecomer to the Story but partner with us in it, offers these words of comfort:

> Not that I have already obtained this or am already perfect, but I press on to make it my own, because Christ Jesus has made me his own. Brothers, I do not consider that I have made it my own. But one thing I do: forgetting what lies behind and straining forward to what lies ahead, I

press on toward the goal for the prize of the upward call of God in Christ Jesus. Let those of us who are mature think this way, and if in anything you think otherwise, God will reveal that also to you. Only let us hold true to what we have attained. Brothers, join in imitating me, and keep your eyes on those who walk according to the example you have in us.[9]

If I might graciously paraphrase, Paul's counsel is something like this: Set your heart on the thing that God set His heart on in the first place—His plan for the fullness of time and your place in it. Make that your one holy passion. If you get off track, God will let you know. Meanwhile, seek out people who've got the Story straight and study how they do it. When it comes to the Story, be humble, diligent, teachable, and available. If you get off script, Yahweh Himself will let you know. That's the safety net and the hope for us who are "flying blind."

ACT V—Consummation: Scene 3 (Revelation)

Here we go, back to the future again. We talked about this when we made a case for the Bible as a narrative, but God really has a funny sense of humor. The Author of our Story decided to make the last scene of His epic narrative the most difficult to decipher. Why do that? As we saw, people approach this mystery with confusion or confidence. How many times have you heard someone talking about Revelation in the language of "cracking a code?" How are we supposed to make sense of God's final installment about His plan for the fullness of time if it must be "unlocked."

Despite what you might get on Google, Revelation cannot be "unveiled." I think we're on dangerous ground when we focus on interpreting Revelation at the expense of understanding its place in Story. Again, remember the faucets: We need biblical (narrative) theology along with systematic (topical). We've worked arduously to birth and nurture a narrative approach to the Bible. Well, we've reached the end of that narrative—Revelation. Its contribution has to fulfill the role of an ending. Even if its complexity means there will not be a complete (or comprehensive) understanding of it on this side of the Resurrection.

So how does the Story end? And what effect should that have on your life and mine?

The full answer to those two questions will occupy the remaining chapters. The short answer is that the Story ends with a masterful conclusion that resolves all the problems created in Act II. The Abrahamic Mission is completed, evidenced by "the nations" singing together around the throne of Yahweh and the Lamb. Then the "credits" roll and time is swallowed up by eternity.

But unlike movie credits that include an exhaustive list of roles, our Story credits are short and sweet. Maybe something like:

> Written and directed by: *Yahweh*
> Starring: *Yeshua Moshiach* (Jesus Messiah)
> Produced by: *The Holy Spirit*

Abraham won't get a nod. Moses won't either. No surprise—neither will you and me. God alone will be glorified. It was *His* plan for the fullness of time to unite all things in Yeshua. Start to finish, it was Yahweh working by grace, in us, through us, and for us, to reverse and restore what Adam had ruined. We have visited this passage before when we talked about sin, but let's go back again:

> Then I saw a new heaven and a new earth, for the first heaven and the first earth had passed away, and the sea was no more. And I saw the holy city, new Jerusalem, coming down out of heaven from God, prepared as a bride adorned for her husband. And I heard a loud voice from the throne saying, "Behold, the dwelling place of God is with man. He will dwell with them, and they will be his people, and God himself will be with them as their God. He will wipe away every tear from their eyes, and death shall be no more, neither shall there be mourning, nor crying, nor pain anymore, for the former things have passed away." And he who was seated on the throne said, *"Behold, I am making all things new."* Also, he said, "Write this down, for these words are trustworthy and true." (Revelation 21:1–5)

"Behold, I am making all things new" summarizes the closing of the Story. It's a preview snapshot of the closing scene, where His grand Story is headed. It's a glorious sight and a blessed hope. The outcome is certain. We *know* how the Story ends! Of course, we have only snippets in this passage—a biblical travel brochure. But we have the end of the Story—and it's amazing. This is a case where a "spoiler" only creates greater anticipation.

But let's stop here and orient ourselves. We might be *longing* for Scene 3, but we are *living* in Scene 2. We are still in the brutal jaws of "the former things." This is the world of tears, death, mourning, crying out, and pain. It is the world of Adam's folly. And ours. It is *this* world that will finally and thoroughly be remade when He makes all things new.

So, what's the point? Or more specifically, what's *my* point? Why are believers still here on earth? How does the Story's *end* give meaning to our lives in the present? Let's go back to Scene 2 to get that "long answer" I was talking about...

16 Adam and Eve Cost Us More Than "Paradise."

When the One Story started, we saw that it wasn't long before everything fell apart. Adam and Eve are familiar to those in the faith family. Their story was the beginning of the "bad news." The "good news" of the gospel is the solution. That means that the Story must be comprehensive enough to make some sense of life for all time, and the gospel must be large enough to be proclaimed to every corner of the universe from which *shalom* has been lost. Remember our definition of *shalom* from the flipside of peace? We start as peace-takers, but once we mature, we are peace-makers. And if my purpose and yours are now inseparable from God's, then it's all intertwined. As we'll see, being a restorer of *shalom* is what it means to be a Story-dweller.

Early in this book, I quoted Cornelius Plantinga, who said that the Old Testament Hebrew word, *shalom,* means "the way things are supposed to be." I claimed that sin's corruption produced the theft of shalom from every facet of life. But now that we know the Story—and our role within it—we need to look in-depth at where *shalom* has been uprooted and what has grown in its place. The more we do that, the more we appreciate the gospel.

There is an epic poem that can be a useful guide in our deep dive into shalom. John Milton's *Paradise Lost* (which many literary critics now consider the greatest English-language poem of all time) is an imagined conversation between Adam and the archangel Michael. In the 10,000-line poem, Milton unpacks in vivid detail what we are calling the One Story. The poem follows Adam on a tour of human corruption. Adam learns of the future murder of his son Abel by his brother Cain in a grisly and lurid portrayal that is as moving as it is accurate.

The Flood, the Tower of Babel, disease, sickness, and death parade themselves before Adam like a lineup of ghastly characters in the drama. The angel Michael walks Adam through the entire Story from the Fall in Eden to the return of Christ—or in our language, Act II through Scene 3 of Act V.

What's the connection? From the poem, we get a deep sense of what was "lost," but ironically, it was not "paradise." It was *shalom*. My point here is that Milton got what happened in Eden right, even if he gave his poem the wrong title. And what happened that day in the Garden has influenced every thread in the fabric of our present lives more than we could ever dream. Sin's corruption became the new normal, and it persists today. This is vital because our understanding of sin sets the trajectory for our entire lives as Christians. To get this wrong is to get it all wrong. So to get it *right* (or close), we will draw on everything we've discussed so far. I know this seems like an overstatement, but it's not. As we bring this book to a close, don't drift off. Stay with me! This is the good stuff. If you are a believer, I want this word—*shalom*—to be burned in your mind. I want it to be natural in your conversation. I want you to teach it to your children so that they might start to understand how it is inseparable from our purpose and our longing for the Kingdom to come.

The Loss of *Shalom* Between Humanity and God

The first (and most obvious) realm where things are not "as they're supposed to be" involves humanity and God. In Eden in Act I, we see a very personal and liberal relationship between God and the two people made in His image. They serve as co-regents, cultivating and protecting the rest of God's creation on His behalf. This was the way things were designed to be. This was "very good." This was shalom.

But sin spoiled that. Suddenly things were *not* "very good." Our First Parents were asked to exit the Garden and were excluded from His presence. They left and so did shalom. This, the most central of all relationships, was vandalized. Suddenly, things between humanity and God were not right, and humanity (sensing this in their souls) has frantically sought to fill the void ever since. Money, sex, and power—the ancient idols that populated Acts II through IV—persist. Because we chase what we value, we eventually worship what we chase in hopes of peace. Unfortunately, what was true for King Solomon is true today. "Things" cannot restore shalom between God and us because "things" are what lured us away in the first place.

The gospel we proclaim is God's appeal to humanity to embrace the remedy He initiated and secured to repair the loss of *shalom* between Him and us. To respond to this offer requires we first admit to being a *shalom*-breaker, a sinner. The Bible calls this repentance. Or, we can reject this offer. The same people who rail *against* God because things aren't as they should be *around* them often refuse to apply the same argument to themselves. And to *refuse* to be reconciled, it would seem, is sin sneaking in the backdoor instead of the front, because it, too, is a disturbance of *shalom:*

> Perhaps we think most often of sin as a spoiler of creation: people adulterate a marriage or befoul a stream or use their excellent minds to devise an ingenious tax fraud. But resistance to redemption counts as sin, too, and often displays a special perversity.[1]

The death of humanity's relationship with its Creator has produced the largest void of all, and it's irreparable unless God intervenes.

Thankfully, He did. As we've seen, Paul spins a theological web connecting the finished work of Christ on Calvary, our justification, God's plan for the fullness of time, and the restoration of *shalom* between God and humanity:

> Therefore, since we have been justified by faith, *we have peace [shalom] with God* through our Lord Jesus Christ. Through him we have also obtained access by faith into this grace in which we stand, and we rejoice in hope of the glory of God. (Romans 5:1–2)

> For in him all the fullness of God was pleased to dwell, and through him to reconcile to himself all things, whether on earth or in heaven, *making peace [shalom] by the blood of his cross"* (Colossians 1:19).

Shalom has been restored, at least substantially, between God and humanity. Its full restoration is in Scene 3 (which we are waiting for!) when the "former things" are truly gone, and God dwells on the new earth. But the fact that the enmity between us and the One whose vandalized image we bear has been restored to *shalom*, even if it's in its infancy, is good news to those who embrace it. It's gospel.

The Loss of *Shalom* Within Humanity

The curtain on Act I closes with the announcement that the "man and woman were both naked and were not ashamed."[2] Although it is a reference to a man and his wife, it is a beautiful portrait of *shalom* within humanity. The absence of fear and the presence of freedom between Adam and Eve is a portrait of how it was supposed to be. But that portrait was also quickly desecrated. Act II inaugurates a stark contrast in interpersonal relationships. Fear and shame—the first to arrive on stage—degenerate to murder and mayhem as Act II unfolds. Fratricide is followed by homicide, and humanity's distrust for itself usurps the place *shalom* once held. As we mentioned earlier, after the Flood, God put a policy of capital punishment in place for capital murder.[3] Apparently, folks weren't getting along too well outside the Garden! James, writing in the first century, indicated nothing had improved by his day:

> What causes quarrels and what causes fights among you? Is it not this, that your passions are at war within you? You desire and do not have, so you murder. You covet and cannot obtain, so you fight and quarrel. You do not have, because you do not ask. You ask and do not receive, because you ask wrongly, to spend it on your passions. (James 4:1–3)

Tragically, this isn't ancient history. We are still immersed in the offspring of Cain's animosity to his brother. It's part of our obsession with "the news." Thanks to the digital age, there is unending access to global atrocities happening in our broken world in real time. The proximity to pain in the headlines and the daily horrors in our newsfeeds have become so commonplace they've somewhat numbed us to human suffering. That is until it arrives at our front door. But even though this "news" is now typical, it's not normal, and it grieves the heart of God.

Then why doesn't He do something about it?

He did. Jesus' death was intended to restore *shalom* between people too. Especially people of different ethnicities. That was part of His plan. The recent division within the evangelical community on issues of race and justice are the rotten fruit of 2D theology. Let's revisit a passage we looked at earlier, but now in the light of ethnic shalomic restoration:

> But now in Christ Jesus you who once were far off have been brought near by the blood of Christ. For *he himself is our peace*, who has made us both one and has broken down in his flesh the dividing wall of hostility by abolishing the law of commandments expressed in ordinances, that he might create in himself one new man in place of the two, *so making*

> *peace*, and might reconcile us both to God in one body through the cross, thereby killing the hostility. And he came and preached *peace* to you who were far off and *peace* to those who were near. (Ephesians 2:13–18)

Four times in six verses, we see the death of Christ did more than restore *shalom* between God and humanity. It set in motion the power for restoration within humanity itself. But by far the clearest and most glorious portrait of what ethnic diversity living in shalomic harmony *could* have looked like in the Garden is this "trailer" from the end of the Story about what it *will* look like:

> After this I looked, and behold, a great multitude that no one could number, from every nation, from all tribes and peoples and languages, standing before the throne and before the Lamb, clothed in white robes, with palm branches in their hands, and crying out with a loud voice, "Salvation belongs to our God who sits on the throne, and to the Lamb!" (Revelation 7:9–10)

God places a huge priority on restoring shalom between those who look like us and those who don't. Our ignorance of this fact has hurt His Church. But, it's not only corporate humanity that has lost shalom. Individuals have as well.

Our Loss of *Shalom* as Individuals

The spoiling of *shalom* means that *each* of us is not as we are supposed to be. Theologians have spilled much ink about this four-syllable malady. They call it *depravity*. Or put in pedestrian terms, every aspect of our lives bears sin's corruptive imprint. And while we may have an extensive library *describing* depravity, we still don't seem to know much on how to *defeat* it. This is truly important because sin turns us against ourselves before it turns us against others. As Plantinga so soberly tells us:

> Sin qualifies as the worst of our troubles because, among other things, it corrupts what is peculiarly human about us. Sin attaches to intention, memory, thought, speech, intelligent action—to all the special features of personhood—and transforms them into weapons.[4]

And because "We are not saved as souls but as wholes,"[5] the restoration of *shalom* has to extend to every area of our being. According to the doctrine of human depravity, sin emptied the vault of *shalom*. Left to ourselves, we are nearly bankrupt when it comes to how we're supposed to be. For example, our mind, the ability to *reason* and trust our conclusions, has been affected by sin. As we read in Ephesians, we are "darkened in our understanding"[6] and can't see life clearly because of sin. There's even a part of us that doesn't *want* to see things the way they're supposed to be.[7] One aspect of our personal shalomic restoration is to allow our minds to be "renewed" by God so we can once again begin to think within the circumference of His plan and purposes in *kairos* time, while living in *chronos*.[8] We have to unlearn the untruths we have accumulated and relearn the truth about God, others, and ourselves.

Sin's assault has also affected our conscience, muddling our ability to *discern* what is right and good from what is not.[9] Our wills, our ability to *choose* what is good, have been crippled.[10] We often find ourselves singing the same dirge Paul lamented about himself:

> For I do not understand my own actions. For I do not do what I want, but I do the very thing I hate. Now if I do what I do not want, I agree with the law, that it is good. So now it is no longer I who do it, but sin that dwells within me. (Romans 7:15–17)

But something even more tangible and painful showcases shalom's absence for us individually—disease and disability. What's your explanation for all the heartache in the world? A lot of people, beloved, blame God. If I had to guess (though there's no way to prove it) our human genome is not what it was when God declared it "very good." We didn't just inherit a sinful nature from Adam; we inherited a genetic map. When it comes to the pains and sufferings in our world, I don't think you need me to catalog the ways our bodies are broken. We see the longing for *shalom* on the psych floors and in the confused faces of loved ones we've lost to Alzheimer's disease. Diabetes, infertility, childhood cancer—these plagues have touched all of us. Our bodies fail and ache. We know something is mortally wrong. Something's missing, and we're beholding what has replaced it.

It should make perfect sense why Yeshua, the "Prince of *Shalom*" in Isaiah's "trailer,"[11] spent half of His life healing bodies. Healing is restoring *shalom*, because the absence of disease is the way things are *supposed* to be. Even the cases of demon possession in the Bible must be understood in this light. The demoniac who mutilated himself and ran around naked is "clothed and in his right mind" after Jesus exorcises the demon. But the account also gives us one very important detail. After the man was healed, he was sitting at the feet of

Jesus. For the first time, *shalom* had returned in its fullness—and he sat.[12]

A man crippled from birth danced. He *didn't* sit.[13] When *shalom* is restored, the shackles of sin's corruption fall off us and we are able to do what we've always wanted, but our bodies prevented. And one day, when Scene 3 arrives, our *bodies* will be restored to their full image-bearing beauty: "Beloved, we are God's children now, and what we will be has not yet appeared; but we know that when he appears we shall be like him, because we shall see him as he is."[14]

Just as God gives us the future hope of a humanity united in worship, He gives us hope of a body functioning perfectly.

> But our citizenship is in heaven, and from it we await a Savior, the Lord Jesus Christ, who will transform our lowly body to be like his glorious body, by the power that enables him even to subject all things to himself. (Philippians 3:20–21)

Understanding the presence of pain and suffering as evidence of shalom's absence doesn't make the pain disappear. But it helps us understand it. And maybe stop blaming God for it. Human suffering is the long half-life of sin's theft of shalom.

The Loss of *Shalom* Between the Rest of Creation and Humanity

We've talked about the eviction of Adam and Eve from the Garden at length, but here's an important detail we haven't mentioned yet: Given what they saw, they didn't *want* to go back.

Again, this is my opinion, but it's based on what Scripture clearly implies. When I picture the Fall, I don't think Adam and Eve ever swallowed the fruit in their mouths. I believe that bite fell from their lips. They gasped, seeing that all around them things were instantly no longer the same. Picture this part of the Story. Instead of conjuring up the cartoon version you heard in Sunday school, *really* try to picture it. What would it look and sound like to have the shalomic harmony of the Garden shattered by sin?

I think it would sound like cries of death and pain—blood, guts, feathers, squealing, and zoological pandemonium as Creation turned on itself. The animals that Adam had calmly interacted with—the animals he named—were suddenly killing one another, trampling vegetation, and even threatening his safety.[15] When God finds Adam and Eve, they're hiding—and afraid. What if their fear wasn't all about guilt? What if they were suddenly painfully aware that they were no longer in charge? And they were scared spitless!

It's logical to assume that animal predation was another fallout of sin.[16] The Garden instantly morphed into Jurassic Park. Adam and Eve became the only two humans in all history who would ever fully understand the power of sin in that way. And because regret is a function of memory not choice, I don't think they ever slept well again.

The loss of *shalom* between living beings and humanity can be found everywhere. Just walk out your front door. From fire ants and mosquitoes to feral pit bulls and coastal sharks, we vacillate between mild irritation and outright paranoia. So, what would Creation look like where shalom was restored?

In Mark's abbreviated account of Jesus' temptation by Satan in the wilderness, he gives a clue. He says Jesus was "with the wild animals."[17] What if this simple aside is a foretaste of the return of *shalom*? Jesus had just successfully faced Satan in the wilderness. I can't picture him then deciding to cower behind a rock, afraid of the "wild animals." I imagine these beasts at ease (even if just temporarily) with the One who had created them.

But there is even clearer evidence in Scripture. The breathtaking "trailers" in Isaiah paint a picture of what Creation looks like when God "makes all things new," when *shalom* is restored on the new earth:

> The wolf shall dwell with the lamb,
> and the leopard shall lie down with the young goat,
> and the calf and the lion and the fattened calf together;
> and a little child shall lead them.
> The cow and the bear shall graze;
> their young shall lie down together;
> and the lion shall eat straw like the ox.
> The nursing child shall play over the hole of the cobra,
> and the weaned child shall put his hand on the adder's den.
> (Isaiah 11:6–8)

It will be breathtaking to experience what Adam once enjoyed; safety and wonder in the presence of God's variegated handiwork. That is Scene 3, the end of the Story. And we (and the beasts) are not the only ones awaiting its return:

> For the creation waits with eager longing for the revealing of the sons of

God. For the creation was subjected to futility, not willingly, but because of him who subjected it, in hope that the creation itself will be set free from its bondage to corruption and obtain the freedom of the glory of the children of God. (Romans 8:19-21)

What the ancients called "earth, wind, and fire" and the unbelieving world knows as "nature" we call Creation. The biblical Creation story presents order and rhythm, dividing and joining, "kinds" and boundaries. We are told that the waves are given limits, beyond which they were not to pass.[18] We savor the remnants of God's artistic love when we watch the sun descend behind a mountain or sink below the ocean at day's end. When we hear the distant surf. When we smell the first fresh air of spring after a long winter. Something deep within us sighs, saying—*This is the way it's supposed to be.*

But it's not always like this. The melodic waves on the shoreline can swell into a hurricane. Winds that rustle the leaves can funnel into a tornado. Creation has not escaped corruption. It, too, can be cruel and heartless because the entire Creation was another victim of sin.

"All Things" Is All Things

There's a well-known story in Mark's Gospel where Jesus is asleep in a boat full of panicked disciples, rowing to keep afloat and alive on a very agitated Sea of Galilee. Upon being rudely and hastily awakened, Jesus turns to the storm and says, "Peace! Quiet yourself!"[19] Two things happened immediately. First, the storm "ceased," and calm returned. Second, his disciples freaked out: "Even the winds and sea obey him." In short, Jesus gave his disciples a taste of shalom, and they were wonderstruck.

I'm not trying to minimize the complexity of disasters on this earth or disagree with the insurance industry that calls them "acts of God." I'm simply suggesting that "natural disasters" are *un*natural disasters. They're expressions of shalom's absence. An expansive understanding of sin demands this courtesy. I want us to keep plunging deeper into the chasm that shalom's departure has created. Why? Because if we're not gripped by just how far humanity fell—and Creation with it—we might spend our lives telling folks, "God loves you and has a wonderful plan for your life . . . pass it on."

Creation can be fun, but it's certainly not safe. At least not anymore, and *not yet*. But neither are we, as we've seen. Put these two together, and we'll have to confess that we haven't been too kind to creation either. I live in a region of the country that has been the poster child for "natural disasters" over the years. Multiple hurricanes and tornados have secured news headlines and presidential visits. Most notably, perhaps, was the Deepwater Horizon disaster in 2010, the largest oil spill in history. It put Alabama in the newsfeeds for a long time. For three months, over 200 million gallons of crude oil was allowed to flow into a small, semitropical area. The fishing industry, wildlife, and general habitats were rocked. Some will never recover. Life, livelihood, and hope were lost, and much of that never made the headlines. Surely this is not the way it was supposed to be.

That accident is just one example. In the words of an aging Native American woman of the Wintu people: "How can the spirit of the earth like the White man? . . . Everywhere the White man has touched it, it is sore."[20]

This may seem like a random quote, but I'm simply suggesting that our treatment of the earth reflects on our spirituality. The world is watching, beloved. The dominion bestowed upon us by God as His co-regents, the charge to "tend" and "guard" the Garden, slowly degenerated into domination. Tending turned to tearing, and protecting turned to pimping, as we have slowly and steadily filled our waterways with trash and our air with particulates and hydrocarbons. This is what sin in humanity has done to God's good earth and everything on it. This is our personal contribution to the spoiling of *shalom*.

> Hear the word of the LORD, O children of Israel,
> for the LORD has a controversy with the inhabitants of the land.
> There is no faithfulness or steadfast love,
> and no knowledge of God in the land;
> There is swearing, lying, murder, stealing, and committing adultery;
> they break all bounds, and bloodshed follows bloodshed.
>
> Therefore the land mourns,
> and all who dwell in it languish,
> and also the beasts of the field
> and the birds of the heavens,
> and even the fish of the sea are taken away. (Hosea 4:1–3)

Even the modern recycling movement, as altruistic as it seems and as good as it makes us feel, belies the fact that we still won't face the uncomfortable truth that consumption (not improper disposal of our waste) is the major cause of pollution. Our desire for more goes back to the Garden. Where does the American church stand when it comes to Creation and its care? Conversations range from ignorance and indifference to animosity and arrogance. Do we view the "earth" as something God gave us, or as something that belongs to Him but He's entrusted into our care? The Scriptures are clear on this: We're tenants on *His* property. We don't own it, despite what the mortgage company says.

Old Testament scholar Sandra Richter asserts that a thoughtful reading of Deuteronomy reveals an amazing consistency by Yahweh regarding His expectations of Israel as "tenants" in Canaan.[21] Among them are attentive and compassionate protection of their livestock, a yearlong rest for the soil, and crop rotation. Even their animals were granted a sabbath each week! Richter calculated the annual cost to the average Jewish household was sixty days' worth of food for obeying Yahweh's order not to "muzzle the ox when he is threshing the grain."[22] This command's full force is buried from our sight because we have no idea what subsistence farming entails. Essentially, Yahweh required His people to care for their beasts in ways that were immensely costly. And this was to be done despite the yield. It wasn't an ancient form of profit-sharing for the animals. It was to be the norm. In fact, we are told in Scripture that how one treated his animals reflected his spirituality: "Whoever is righteous has regard for the life of his beast, but the mercy of the wicked is cruel."[23] Yahweh even expected His people to hunt differently than their pagan neighbors. If a mother and its eggs were found together, both could not be taken.

And that wasn't all. Yahweh forbade the Jews from destroying fruit-bearing trees of their enemies when besieging a city. This was in direct contrast to the military tactics of their neighboring enemies, the Egyptians and Assyrians. Fruit devastation was the surest way to destroy the economy of an enemy. The psychological effect of witnessing the destruction of trees that were in your family for centuries was a profound weapon by itself. Yahweh forbade it.

Please don't jump ship here. I'm not promoting being "green." What I am suggesting is so much deeper than that, and it goes back to the very beginning of this book. I'm not talking about taking up a banner or a cause. Our very mindsets must be transformed—turned outward. Beyond our blurry, parochial self-interest. Beyond our consumption. If we are Creationists to any degree (people who believe that God is the source of everything visible and invisible), then to embrace any view of creation that does *not* honor and obey the Creator is sin. In fact, for you and me to live in such a way is to *spoil* shalom.

I am also trying to help us begin to understand what's really happening when humanity misuses and abuses creation. We know the Story now. We know what creation was, what it's become, and what it will be again. To live inconsistently with that knowledge is willful rebellion.

In 1970, Francis Schaeffer, a prophet everyone wanted to read but no one wanted to heed, penned *Pollution and the Death of Man: A Christian View of Ecology*. I'll never forget reading it. I was a new believer *and* an environmental research chemist. Schaeffer was arguing for Christians to take the lead on this issue based on our *theology*, not our pocketbooks. And, of particular interest to the point we're making in this book, Schaeffer linked creation care to redemption:

> On the basis of the fact that there is going to be total redemption in the future, not only of man but of all creation, the Christian who believes the Bible should be the man who—with God's help and in the power of the Holy Spirit—is treating nature now in the direction of the way nature will be then. It will not now be perfect, but there should be something substantial or we have missed our calling. God's calling to the Christian now, and to the Christian community, in the area of nature (just as it is in the area of personal Christian living in true spirituality) is that we should exhibit a substantial healing here and now, between man and nature and nature and itself, as far as Christians can bring it to pass.[24]

Long before environmentalism was politicized, Schaeffer made a passionate plea to the Church to have an expansive understanding of redemption—large enough to include everything in life that wasn't the way it was supposed to be. One that has room for everything that's broken. A redemption—a restoration of shalom—which extends, in the words of the popular Christmas carol, "far as the curse is found."[25]

At the end of the One Story, when God Himself, speaking from the throne in Scene 3 of Act V, says, "Behold, I make all things new," we need to know what He means by "all things." I suspect that by this point, we agreed that the *absence* of shalom is owed to the *presence* of sin, and "all things" must refer to everything that sin has infected. This means "all things" is everything from which shalom has been banished. Therefore, "all things" *is* all things.

It's no coincidence that in the final moments of the Story, a city representing the entire story of redemption descends from heaven to the new earth. Its name is *Jeru-shalom*, "vision of peace." The Story concludes with the passing away of the "former things" and the restoration of shalom. That means the loss of shalom and its restoration to the glory of God *is* the Story!

One Point Has Many Possibilities

The Abrahamic Mission, the "blessing of the nations," the restoration of shalom, is the mission of every Christian. Those who have been restored to shalom with God, who are beneficiaries of His grace, have also been enlisted to be agents of His redemption. If we refuse to be agents of shalomic restoration (in *all* the areas where it is missing) it is because we are either rebellious or ignorant. And if you've read this far, the second option is off the table.

To be a Story-dweller is to be a shalom-restorer. It is the purpose of my justification. My peace with God becomes the starting point for me to be a restorer of peace as a member of God's new family.

This is what Jesus meant when He said, "Blessed are the peace *[shalom]* makers, for they shall be called sons of God."[26] Proclaiming to people that God has made a way for them to be restored to shalom with Him, and that He has a place for them in His shalom-restoring enterprise, is the "good news," the gospel. The gospel has always been centrifugal, moving out *from* ourselves, instead of inward, *for* ourselves:

> For if we are beside ourselves, it is for God; if we are in our right mind, it is for you. For the love of Christ controls us, because we have concluded this: that one has died for all, therefore all have died; and *he died for all, that those who live might no longer live for themselves but for him* who for their sake died and was raised. (2 Corinthians 5:13–15)

"Not living for ourselves, but for him who for our sake died and was raised," is what Jesus called "losing" our lives for His sake and the gospel.[27] For those who understand *who* they are, and the Story that explains *why* they are, it means that the possibilities for participating in the restoration of shalom are as expansive as the reach of sin and as varied as humanity itself. And God assures us that in the process, we, too, will be transformed.

I'm sorry if I sound like a voice loop here, but I'm going to say it again: My own spiritual transformation is a byproduct of my participation in the Abrahamic Mission, *not* the result of spiritual self-focus. Our spirituality is inseparably bound to the restoration of shalom *for others*: "But seek the welfare *[shalom]* of the city where I have sent you into exile, and pray to the LORD on its behalf, for in its welfare *[shalom]* you will find your welfare *[shalom]*."[28]

Those in His Story are at vastly different stages. Some of us are at the beginning of life's longest chapter. Marriage, first career, raising a family are the typical concentric circles of this season, and they're beginning to work their way outward. The opportunities for restoring shalom in these circles should excite you because they are limitless!

Pastors and church leaders have one of the most fulfilling jobs — and the most exhausting. These vocations are the most obvious vehicles of shalom-restoration, but some people are in the shalom-restoring business whether they realize it or not.

Our twin daughters are nurses, and the stories they have shared with Jill and me over the years have taken our breath away. Our daughter Heather once told me that she feels like God has given her "the gift of life." She actually had a patient say those very words as she was starting her twelve-hour shift. People recognize shalom when they receive it even though they don't know what to call it, or realize it issues from the heart of God Himself.

On my podcast, I have interviewed dear friends who are also full-time shalom-restorers. One of them that comes to mind is in palliative care. Holding the hand of the dying could not be closer to the heart of Christ. But you don't have to be a frontline medical worker in a pandemic to be restoring shalom. The thrill of this Christian life is that once our eyes are open, the opportunities are unlimited. Since sharing some of these concepts, I have had a renowned orthopedic surgeon tell me that his entire life's work now has new meaning. He's doing more than just fixing a torn meniscus and earning a paycheck. He gets to be a part of pushing back the shadows. Of *healing.* That is the byproduct of sitting in the Great Examiner's chair. Of letting him click the focus of our lives into place. And the examples are veritably endless. Committed parents who instill in their growing children a sense of wonder over the kairotic purposes of God through being foster parents. Guiding their children to discover that unique niche for them in the One Story. Youth pastors who expose their students to urban and rural poverty, educational inequities in their cities, and the shalomic vacuums they can pour substantial grace into. I even look back on my own years as a research chemist, laboring sometimes 30 days straight without time off, pouring over solutions to what we'd done to America's waterways via pollution. Even without realizing it, nearly fifty years ago, I was working for shalomic restoration for God's Creation.

The restoration of *shalom* should also be a litmus test for churches when it comes to setting budgets, implementing curricula and programs, and forging theologies of church growth.

In our Christian schools, it is the same. We need to instill an understanding of the Story *and* equip children to find their place in it. As a teacher, I got to witness the miracle that came from pairing high school students (who were often steeped in 2D theology) with *shalom*-restoring programs within our city. Crisis pregnancy centers, urban ministries, special needs programs, tutoring, reading initiatives, and Habitat for Humanity were among the partnerships. I was front-row for the soul awakening that came from face-to-face ministry to people in need. Once involved in shalomic restoration, you come to life. When the urban child you've been tutoring considers you her best friend …when the special needs child smiles at your joke…when the hands of the hungry woman cup the food you have served her—you find your role as part of the solution. And it is addicting.

It should go without saying that without understanding the Story and without the Holy Spirit, encountering places where shalom is lost will terrify or cripple us. My daughter Havilah teaches nursing, so she, too, gets to witness young people (many of them very sheltered) experience what I have just described. But some of them can't handle it. At least not at first.

This brings us back to the fact that we are broken vessels. That only Yahweh can (and will) bring ultimate restoration. We are in Scene 2, longing for Scene 3—but we are driven by Acts II and IV. This means we don't focus on the future to the detriment of the present. There is something we can do—right now. We were *meant* to do this. The Story is pulling us in!

17 Would You Recognize Jesus If You Met Him?

I've said numerous times that sanctification is becoming less and less like Adam and more and more like Jesus. I call the process God's "Great Reversal." Have you ever wondered why God's plan for each of us is to resemble Jesus? Yahweh is so committed to this transformation that He's predestined it for each of us in His new family. We also are given His motivation for this cataclysmic change in our nature:

> And we know that for those who love God all things work together for good, for those who are called according to his purpose. For those whom he foreknew he also predestined to be conformed to the image of his Son, *in order that* he might be the firstborn among many brothers. (Romans 8:28–29)

And Paul would know what this means better than anyone. When first encountered the risen and ascended Jesus on the road to Damascus, Jesus asked Paul, "Why are you persecuting me?" Don't miss this. Jesus was equating the young Church Paul was persecuting to himself. You hurt them, you hurt Jesus. Why?

We are his body. His physical presence in the modern world. Paul says God is in the business of transforming us to resemble Jesus so that He'll have more "Jesuses," in a sense. So that Jesus would be the "firstborn among many family members."

The traditional teaching about Jesus Christ uses titles like prophet, priest, and king to describe his various roles in redemption. These are beautiful, but they almost always get caught in the suction of two-dimensional theology (the personal and parochial benefits). I'd like to introduce another major role in the Story that Jesus fulfilled while on earth. One that has everything to do with the Abrahamic Mission and the restoration of shalom. And one that is at the heart of our spiritual transformation into his likeness. That of an "advocate." Let me show you what I mean.

In a dialogue between Yahweh and Abraham in Genesis 18, where Abraham is advocating for mercy for the sin-choked city where his nephew Lot lives, Yahweh makes a magnificent statement:

> The LORD said, "Shall I hide from Abraham what I am about to do, seeing that Abraham shall surely become a great and mighty nation, and all the nations of the earth shall be blessed in him? For I have chosen him, that he may command his children and his household after him *to keep the way of the LORD by doing righteousness and justice*, so that the LORD may bring to Abraham what he has promised him." Then the LORD said, "Because the outcry against Sodom and Gomorrah is great and their sin is very grave . . ." (Genesis 18:17–19)

It's worth noting this word for "outcry" is not a little call for help—it's in the same word family as when a woman is being raped. It was the word used by the Jews when they were trapped between the Red Sea and Pharaoh's armed forces. It's the word for the unheeded cry of the poor and perishing. And what is Yahweh's response to it? Righteousness and justice.

Those groups from whom an "outcry" is most likely are mentioned over 260 times in over half of the books in our Bibles. "The widow," "the fatherless," "the afflicted," "the oppressed," "the refugee," "the weak," and "the poor" are distinct people groups in the eyes and heart of Yahweh. They are not social problems to be solved by governmental agencies.

One inescapable truth from this passage is that Yahweh *chose* Abraham for "doing righteousness and justice" and that doing so is synonymous with "keeping the way of the LORD."

"Doing righteousness" is the way or path of the Lord. So, when we inherit Abraham's blessing, we are tasked with the mission that went with it—the mission of advocacy for others. Righteousness and justice are blessings, but they are to emanate *from* us, not just *to* us.

But the Abrahamic Mission seems to have been hijacked by the American Dream. And Speaking of the American Dream, there was a guy in the Bible who seemed to have achieved the ancient equivalent. He had it all. Great family, sound investments, a great retirement plan. You name it; he had it. And then he lost it. All of it, in a single day.

You know this man as Job. So let me ask you, what are the first words that come to mind when you hear his name? I bet they're something like pain and suffering, and ultimately, perseverance. But did you know that the praise God gave to Job had nothing to do with suffering and his Olympian endurance? Yahweh praised Job *before* the pain began. According to God, Job was "blameless and upright." He "feared God" and walked away from evil. God goes so far as to say in the face of Satan himself that there was "no one else" like Job. He says it *twice* before the bottom falls out of Job's life![1] And keep in mind that this is an ancient tale told in an *oral* culture. The audience would have known of Job's innocence even before his suffering began, making the account about Job much more than an epic saga about undaunted courage or undying love.

So what *was* so special about Job before the tsunami of pain arrived? What caused God to say He had no one like him? The answers to those questions are buried in Job's journal entry chronicling the days before his world imploded. And from this entry, we discover Job was living a life of advocacy:

> When the ear heard, it called me blessed, and when the eye saw, it approved, because I delivered the poor who cried for help, and the fatherless who had none to help him. The blessing of him who was about to perish came upon me, and I caused the widow's heart to sing for joy. I put on *righteousness*, and it clothed me; my *justice* was like a robe and a turban. I was eyes to the blind and feet to the lame. I was a father to the needy, and I searched out the cause of him whom I did not know. I broke the fangs of the unrighteous and made him drop his prey from his teeth. (Job 29:11–17)

In the opening verses, Yahweh is praising Job for his passion for *ministry*, not his perseverance in *misery*. We know this because He praised him *before* He tested him. Job is living proof of what God values more than sacrifice—*mercy*.[2]

From Job, let's jump to the ultimate advocate—Jesus. The life and teaching of Yeshua provide our penultimate portrait of an advocate. Jesus opens and closes His earthly ministry with references to advocacy—both His *and* ours. He uses advocacy as proof that the Kingdom has come with his arrival and that, in a very surprising way, advocacy becomes a litmus test for who's in that Kingdom and who isn't. Let's start with Yeshua's ministry debut.

I want to revisit something we looked at briefly about eleven chapters ago. It's an episode in Luke's Gospel that marks Jesus's self-disclosure as the Messiah. Scholars call it "The Nazareth Manifesto." His first public sermon of record was fewer than two hundred words in length, nearly a third of which he borrowed from Isaiah. But Luke tells us that Jesus intentionally searched for this message. Imagine Jesus unrolling a scroll of papyrus covered with Hebrew words that lacked page numbers, chapter numbers, and verse numbers. A scroll of one long, unbroken paragraph. He unrolls it, his finger tracing until He finds the passage Yahweh had led Him to read:

> The Spirit of the Lord is upon me,
> because he has anointed me
> to proclaim good news to the poor.
> He has sent me to proclaim liberty to the captives
> and recovering of sight to the blind
> to set at liberty those who are oppressed,
> to proclaim the year of the Lord's favor.
> (Luke 4:16–19, cf. Isaiah 61:1–4)

Then, to everyone's amazement (including His family's), Jesus says this passage is referring to *himself!* Jesus affirms that the arrival of the Messiah is "good news" *for the poor*. The Jews who were present would have immediately done a mental sweep. They would have known the context. All that came before and after the verses Yeshua read. And they would have found themselves face to face with language that had to do with the end of oppression and sorrow for those helpless to help themselves. This event in a small synagogue in Nazareth marked the debut of the One who *will*, as the Scriptures tell us, "Walk in the ways of the LORD" and "do righteousness and justice on the earth." This was not a carpenter's son in a synagogue. This was Yahweh in a body! The intersection of heaven and earth that was once the tabernacle, and then the temple, was now standing in their midst. And as Yahweh in a body stepped onto the stage that had been two thousand years in the making, His first pronouncement as the King who has come, was that God had "anointed" (the root word for

Messiah) Him to bring "good news" *to the poor.* Don't miss this. You must not miss this. They did. And in doing so, they missed Yeshua too.

Jump now to the end of His earthly ministry. In a flurry of questions from his disciples about his return, Jesus jumps ahead to the final significant event just before the end of the One Story—the final judgment. The barometer Yahweh uses to determine (or verify) intimacy with Him—who knew Him and who did not—should sound familiar, but hopefully more personal and profound than you have heard it in the past:

> Before him will be gathered all the nations, and he will separate people one from another as a shepherd separates the sheep from the goats. And he will place the sheep on his right, but the goats on the left. Then the King will say to those on his right, "Come, you who are blessed by my Father, inherit the kingdom prepared for you from the foundation of the world. For I was hungry and you gave me food, I was thirsty and you gave me drink, I was a stranger and you welcomed me, I was naked and you clothed me, I was sick and you visited me, I was in prison and you came to me." Then the righteous will answer him, saying, "Lord, when did we see you hungry and feed you, or thirsty and give you drink? And when did we see you a stranger and welcome you, or naked and clothe you? And when did we see you sick or in prison and visit you?" And the King will answer them, "Truly, I say to you, as you did it to one of the least of these my brothers, you did it to me." (Matthew 25:32–40)

In a sense, Yeshua's criteria for this entrance interview is whether an individual had lived as an "advocate." Or put another way, whether they had lived like Job. Whether or not they had fulfilled the Abrahamic Mission. Whether or not they were shalom-makers. After all, it's the family business.

As we end now, I hope it's obvious why I've repeatedly said that the gospel is *not* "God loves you and has a wonderful plan for your life." Let me reword that significantly and say that the gospel *is,* "God has a plan for the fullness of time to unite all things in heaven and earth in Yeshua the Messiah, and He has a wonderful *place* for your life in it."

The Story is big, but I hope that doesn't deter you from sharing it. We should be awestruck but not overwhelmed. The details I've given along the way are to prove to you that the Story is worthy of a life of study. Wherever you are on this journey, beloved, don't be discouraged. He meets us where we are. By His

Spirit—there is always something for us in His Word. You don't have to know every facet of this Story to share the good news! And the first step in sharing is being the instrument of shalom like we have been talking about. It is being like your Father, *El Roi*—the God Who Sees. It is *seeing* the hurting and letting that occupy your thoughts. Not your grocery lists, or your beach vacation, or the crabgrass in your lawn.

Since the first version of this book came out a decade ago, I started a podcast. I called it *The Road to Shalom*. To me, it was a decent mission statement on what we are doing in this Christian life. So let me close with a question. I've asked it on the podcast and countless other times during my ministry. Every time I do, the room falls quiet:

What do you want to hear from God the day you meet Him?

Take a minute and really formulate an answer. Okay, let's push that question a little further. Most believers want to hear God say, "Well done my good and faithful servant. Enter into the joy of your Father." To be honest, that's what I'd want to hear myself.

But what if *we* have to speak first? What is the only reasonable thing you could say to *God* that would cause Him to say to *you*, "Well done…?"

It can't be anything related to gratitude or praise or being forgiven. There's only one thing you can say to God when you meet Him that would elicit that response. It's the same thing Jesus said to his Father shortly before the crucifixion: "I have glorified you on earth by completing the work you gave me to do."[3]

Life really is a river. It is the torrent of grace, and the Story is calling you in. True evangelizing means pulling others in with you. The river is where we find meaning, not sitting on the banks waiting for "heaven." In some ways, this book is my love letter to the American Church I've given much of my time and teaching to. My commitment to the gospel of grace has not wavered. Woe to any who would try to "work" their way "in"—*it's by grace alone, through faith alone, in Christ alone*. There is no chorus that we should more loudly sing.

But there is work for you to do while you're here, beloved. That's the flipside of the grace that justified me, as we saw at the beginning. Paul said it best, "…and his grace toward me was not in vain. On the contrary, I worked harder than any of them, though it was not I, but the grace of God that is with me."[4] And in my old age, I must boldly say this. I have seen too many depressed, dissatisfied, lost young Christians who have no idea that their sanctification is not *for* them. With your blessing comes a mission. It is a thrill and an honor and the whisper in your very soul. Put down this book and, like Paul, fall to your knees.

Now that you know the Story, I'll ask you the question I asked in the beginning: *Beloved, have you been trying to squeeze God into your story, or are you finding your place in His, the One Story of the One God?*

Notes

INTRODUCTION: *The One Story And Why We Need It Now*
1 Statement by protagonist, Peter Wyett in Charles Martin's, *Unwritten.* (New York: Center Street-Hatchett Book Group, 2013), 5.

CHAPTER 1: Learning To See Out of Both Eyes
1 Auden, W.H. *Collected Poems.* Reprint Edition. (New York: Vintage), 1991.
2 Jeffrey Bilbro. *Reading the Times - A Theological and Literary Inquiry into The News.* (Downers Grove: InterVarsity Press, 2021), 69.
3 Galatians 4:4
4 John 1:14, *The Message.* Eugene H. Peterson, (Colorado Springs: NavPress, 2002)
5 Cf. Ephesians 1:3, 20; 2:6; 3:10; 6:12
6 David Lyle Jeffrey, *People of the Book: Christian Identity and Literary Culture.* (Grand Rapids, MI: 1996), 26. Cited by Bilbro, 92.
7 Bilbro, 67.
8 Romans 11:33–34
9 Colossians 1:26
10 Wayne Grudem. *Bible Doctrine: Essential Teachings of the Christian Faith.* (Grand Rapids: Zondervan, 1999), 17.
11 (adapted from) Edward Klink and Darian Lockett. *Understanding Biblical Theology-A Comparison of Theory and Practice.* (Grand Rapids: Zondervan, 2012), 22–25.

CHAPTER 2: Four-Dimensional Faith
1 14.3 billion hits for "sin"; 4.7 billion for "Jesus"; last accessed 3/19/22
2 Romans 3:23
3 Romans 5:12
4 Isaiah 11:6–8; 66:25
5 Revelation 21:5
6 Mark 10:45

CHAPTER 3: PEACE: "All Ya Need is Love"...Not!
1 Richie Utenburger, *Eight Miles High: Folk-Rock's Flight from Haight-Ashbury to Woodstock.* (Kindle edition, 2015), 228.
2 Romans 5:1
3 John 14:27
4 Ephesians 2:14
5 Cornelius Plantinga Jr., *Not the Way It's Supposed to Be: A Breviary of Sin.* (Grand Rapids: Eerdmans, 1995). A study of the nature of sin, including corruption, deceit, folly, addiction, attacks on God, and flight from God.
6 Genesis 37:4
7 Amos 5:19
8 Galatians 3:28
9 I Peter 3:11

10 Jeremiah 29:7
11 Matthew 5:9
12 Ephesians 2:8–9

CHAPTER 4: GRACE: More Amazing Than You Know
1 Ephesians 2:7
2 Ephesians 1:7–8; 2:7
3 Romans 3:22–24
4 Romans 12:6
5 2 Corinthians 9:8
6 Ephesians 4:29

CHAPTER 5: RIGHTEOUSNESS: Getting it "Right."
1 Galatians 3:28–29
2 Proverbs 10:11
3 Jeremiah 23:5
4 Romans 2:13, NIV
5 Matthew 6:1–2
6 Matthew 9:13
7 2 Corinthians 5:21
8 John 5:17
9 John 14:12
10 Genesis 16:13; Exodus 15:26
11 Matthew 5:16
12 James 3:18
13 Romans 12:1

CHAPTER 6: SANCTIFICATION: Transformed for a Purpose
1 See for example, John Owen, *The Mortification of Sin (Puritan Paperbacks)*. (Banner of Truth Trust, 2004); R.C. Sproul. *Growing in Holiness: Understanding God's Role and Yours*, (Grand Rapids: Baker Books, 2020); N.T. Wright. *After You Believe: Why Christian Character Matters*, (New York: HarperOne, 2012).
2 1 Corinthians 1:2
3 Romans 6:22
4 Gal. 5:22–23
5 Romans 8:29
6 Philippians 3:12
7 Grudem, p.758
8 Titus 2:14
9 2 Timothy 2:21

CHAPTER 7: What's the Story on the One Story?
1 Bilbro, 85.
2 "Koheleth" is from a Hebrew word that appears seven times in Ecclesiastes, translated "Preacher" (ESV, KJV) or "Teacher" (NIV).

3   The literal Hebrew title of Ecclesiastes is "The Words of Qoheleth, the son of David, king in Jerusalem."
4   Gordon Dahl, *Work, Play, and Worship in a Leisure-Oriented Society* (Minneapolis: Augsburg Press, 1972), 12.
5   "Take it Easy," *The Eagles*, Asylum Records, 1972
6   https://www.csmedia1.com/paseodelrey.org/continuous-partial-attention.pdf (last accessed: 3/31/22)
7   Carr, *The Shallows*, 165.
8   Ibid, 166.

CHAPTER 8: What Is the Bible…Really?
1   Eugene Peterson, *The Pastor: A Memoir* (San Francisco: Harper One, 2011), 248–49.

CHAPTER 9: "Let's Work Our Way Backwards"
1   Revelation 22:8
2   Philippians 2:8–11
3   Psalm 78
4   Christopher J. H. Wright, *The Mission of God's People: A Biblical Theology of the Church's Mission* (Grand Rapids: Zondervan, 2010), 101.
5   On Paul's teaching on godliness, cf. 1 Timothy 2:2; 3:16; 4:7–8; 6:3, 5–6, 11; 2 Timothy 3:5; Titus 1:1.
6   Matthew 6:19–20
7   Matthew 25:14–30
8   I Cor. 3:15

CHAPTER 10: New Eyes, Not Better Glasses
1   For example, it is clear from Luke 9:26–27 that when the early church refused to entertain the possibility that Saul had come to faith, Barnabas sought him out and listened to his story. He risked his life in doing so and undoubtedly forged a bond that would characterize their relationship for many years.
2   Acts 9:36–10:23
3   Isaiah 42:6 and 19
4   2 Corinthians 3:12–16
5   Colossians 1:24–28
6   2 Peter 1:16–20
7   Ephesians 1:9; 3:3,4,9; 5:32; 6:19
8   On the mystery of Christ, cf. Ephesians 1:4; Revelation 13:8; 1 Corinthians 15:22,45; Colossians 1:19–20.
9   Galatians 4:4–5
10 Exodus 33:13
11 Psalm 103:7
12 Exodus 33:11
13 John 15:15
14 Romans 11:33

CHAPTER 11: The Power of the Gospel: Narrative or Imperative?
1. Acts 20:24
2. Matthew 27:51
3. Galatians 3:8
4. Philippians 3 contains Paul's most detailed description of his resume *outside* the Story, *and* his dismissal of it in contrast to simply being *in* the One Story.
5. Luke's description in Acts 9:1, combined with Paul's own confessional sorrow elsewhere in Acts, creates a very strong case for violence and murder at his hands (cf. Acts 22:3–4; 26:9–11; Galatians 1:13).
6. See 1 Corinthians 15:10 and 2 Corinthians 11:23–29.
7. Galatians 4:19
8. Annie Dillard, "The Book of Luke," in *The Annie Dillard Reader* (New York: HarperCollins, 1994), 266.

CHAPTER 12: ACTS I – III: Commencement, Conflict, Complication
1. N. T. Wright, *Simply Jesus* (San Francisco: HarperOne, 2011).
2. Genesis 1:28, 31; 5:1–2
3. cf. Genesis 9:6
4. Galatians 3:7–9, 27–29
5. On prophetic confrontation of the sins of kings, cf. 2 Kings 20:12–21 and 1 Kings 21:20–26.
6. Jeremiah 2:13
7. Robert Van Kampen, *The Sign* (Wheaton, IL: Crossway, 1992), 243–44.
8. On Jesus addressing the "last days," cf. Matthew 24:1–4; Mark 13:3–5.
9. cf. Acts 1:6–8
10. cf. John 21:18–23
11. cf. Philippians 4:11–13

CHAPTER 13: Intermission: The Story's "Missing Page"
1. The actual length of this "blank page" era is disputed among scholars, largely because of the difficulty in ascribing exact dates to the events recorded in Ezra and Nehemiah. We must remind ourselves that we are *not* seeking to create a time *line*, but rather a time *window* in which God was "silent" from the prophetic standpoint.
2. See John 21:25
3. See Ezra 1:1–66 and Isaiah 44:28.
4. Acts 18:24–28;
5. Acts 6:8ff
6. Acts 28:11–16
7. Acts 22:25–29; 23:27
8. Galatians 4:4; Paul's use of *pleroma* ("fullness") here denotes something being completed, similar to a container finally being "full."
9. John the Baptist opens ACT IV: Mark 1:1–3; John 1:19–23; cf. Isaiah 40:3.

CHAPTER 14: ACT IV — Climax
1. John 21:25
2. Matthew 2:1,11; Luke 2:8–20, 25–38

3 Cf. John 2:19; Matthew 12:6
4 Mark 1:1, 14–15
5 Mark 1:4; Luke 1:76–77; 3:1; 24:45–47
6 Matthew 4:23; 9:35; 11:5; 24:14; Luke 7:22; 9:6
7 cf. Matthew 28:20
8 Paul mentions Abraham nineteen times, compared to nine mentions of Moses
9 John 8:56
10 cf. Isaiah 61:1–3 and Luke 4:16–19
11 Luke 4:21; Jesus' comment in the perfect tense in Greek. He is speaking here of a very permanent "fulfillment."
12 N. T. Wright, *Simply Jesus: A New Vision of Who He Was, What He Did, and Why It Matters* (San Francisco: Harper One, 2011), 90–91.
13 cf. 1 Kings 1:33–35
14 cf. Zechariah 9:9
15 cf. John 12:31–33
16 John 12:31
17 On confusion about Jesus' mission, cf. Luke 17:18–20; Mark 14:3–11; Matthew 20:20–28.
18 John 19:30
19 John 17:1–5
20 See Mark 16:19; Ephesians 1:20; 1 Peter 3:22; Hebrews 1:3
21 Revelation 21:5
22 John 14:12
23 Mark 10:45; See also Matthew 20:26–28; Luke 22:26–27; Titus 2:14
24 On the inseparable nature of Jesus' messianic ministry and his tending to physical need, cf. Matthew 4:23; 9:35; 11:2–6; Luke 4:16–21.
25 Romans 8:29
26 cf. John 14:12

CHAPTER 15: ACT V — Culmination
1 John 14:9
2 Hebrews 1:3
3 Christopher J. H. Wright, *The Mission of God* (Downers Grove, IL: IVP Academic, 2006), 62.
4 Christopher J. H. Wright, *The Mission of God's People: A Biblical Theology of the Church's Mission* (Grand Rapids: Zondervan, 2010), 93.
5 See 2 Peter 3:14–16
6 See, for example: Acts 16:6–9
7 Galatians 3:26–29; 1 Corinthians 6:7–11
8 1 Peter 5:5
9 Philippians 3:12–17

CHAPTER 16: Adam and Eve Cost Us More Than "Paradise."
1 Cornelius Plantinga, *Not the Way It's Supposed to Be: A Breviary of Sin*, (Grand Rapids: Eerdmans, 1996), 8.
2 Genesis 2:25
3 cf. Genesis 9:6

4   Plantinga, 76.
5   N. T. Wright, *Surprised by Hope: Rethinking Heaven, the Resurrection, and the Mission of the Church* (San Francisco: Harper One, 2008), 199.
6   Ephesians 4:18
7   Romans 7–8; Colossians 1:21–22.
8   Romans 12:1–2
9   Hebrews 5:14
10 On the full effects of sin, cf. Titus 1:15 and Hebrews 5:15; Romans 7:14–24 and Philippians 2:12–13.
11 Isaiah 9:6
12 Luke 8:35
13 Acts 3:1–8
14 1 John 3:2
15 Genesis 2:18–20
16 The Genesis account is clear that everything that had breath ate vegetation when things were as they were supposed to be (Genesis 1:29–30). The emergence of "thorns and thistles" as part of the curse on the earth suggests a change in the plant genome (Genesis 3:17–18). A parallel change within the animal kingdom is equally plausible.
17 Mark 1:13. The word translated, "with" means "amidst" or "in accompaniment with." The word for "animal" is only used of dangerous animals, predators.
18 Job 38:4–11; Genesis 1:1–9
19 Mark 4:35–41
20 *Touch The Earth: A Self-Portrait of Indian Existence*, comp. T. C. McLuhan (New York: Promontory Press, 1971), 15.
21 The ideas in this section are from Sandra Richter, "Environmental Law in Deuteronomy: One Lens on a Biblical Theology of Creation Care," *Bulletin for Biblical Research* 20, no. 3 (2010): 355–76.
22 Deuteronomy 25:4
23 Proverbs 12:10
24 Francis Schaeffer and Udo Middelmann, *Pollution and the Death of Man: A Christian View of Ecology* (Wheaton, IL: Tyndale House, 1970), 39–40.
25 Isaac Watts' "Joy to the World" is a song about Jesus' *return*, not his birth. The chorus at the end of the first stanza, "Let heaven and nature sing," comes very close to a biblical understanding of Scene 3.
26 cf. Matthew 5:9
27 Mark 8:35
28 Jeremiah 29:7

CHAPTER 17: Would You Recognize Jesus If You Met Him?

1   Job 1:8; 2:3
2   cf. Hosea 6:6; Matthew 9:13
3   John 17:4
4   1 Corinthians 15:10

More "One Story" Resources at fransciacca.com

Study the One Story Itself! (self-study Bible courses)

Fran's 3-part biblical literacy series for personal or small group use.

The 15/30 Series (devotional guides)

Four devotional Bible studies that will provide you with just enough guidance and a whole lot of liberty for you to spend time alone in the Scriptures in a devotional frame of mind.

"What's Wrong With the World?"

This 14-episode video series created for group settings, introduces people to the One Story and invite them to find their place in it.

"Knot or Noose? – Recovering the Mystery of Marriage"

This 9-episode video series carries the major ideas of Have We Lost the Plot? into the world of marriage. An excellent resource for home groups, Sunday school classes, and premarital counseling sessions.